FABULOUS
PAINTED PROJECTS
for the Home

FABULOUS
PAINTED PROJECTS
for the Home

Sterling Publishing Co., Inc. New York
A Sterling/Chapelle Book

Chapelle, Ltd.:

If you have any questions or comments, please contact:

Chapelle, Ltd., Inc., P.O. Box 9252,

Ogden, UT 84409

(801) 621-2777 • (801) 621-2788 Fax

e-mail: chapelle@chapelleltd.com

Web site: www.chapelleltd.com

Plaid, Inc.:

If you have any questions or comments, contact:

Plaid Enterprises, Inc.

Norcross, GA 30091-7600

(800) 842-4197 • Web site: plaidonline.com

Library of Congress Cataloging-in-Publication Data

10 9 8 7 6 5 4 3 2 1
Published by Sterling Publishing Co., Inc.
387 Park Ave. South, New York, NY 10016
©2005 By Plaid
Distributed in Canada by Sterling Publishing
c/o Canadian Manda Group, 165 Dufferin St.
Toronto, Ontario, Canada M6K 3H6
Distributed in Great Britain by Chrysalis Books Group PLC,
The Chrysalis Building, Bramley Road, London W10 6SP, England
Distributed in Australia by Capricorn Link (Australia) Pty. Ltd.
P. O. Box 704, Windsor, NSW 2756, Australia
Printed and Bound in China
All Rights Reserved

Sterling ISBN 1-4027-1751-2
For information about custom editions, special sales, premium
and corporate purchases, please contact Sterling Special Sales
Department at 800-805-5489 or specialsales@sterlingpub.com

Special thank-you to the Artists.

Plaid Enterprises, Inc., prides itself in having a team of the best artists in the country. These artists teach across the country, appear on television, demonstrate at trade shows, contribute to magazines, and help promote the FolkArt line of paint. Plaid is most grateful to the wonderful group of artists who shared their painting knowledge and contributed their projects to make this book possible.

The copy, photographs, and designs in this volume are intended for the personal use of the reader and may be reproduced for that purpose only. Any other use, especially commercial use, is forbidden under law without the written permission of the copyright holder.

Every effort has been made to ensure that all information in this book is accurate. However, due to differing conditions, tools, and individual skills, the publisher cannot be responsible for any injuries, losses, and/or other damages, which may result from the use of the information in this book.

This volume is meant to stimulate decorating ideas. If readers are unfamiliar or not proficient in a skill necessary to attempt a project, we urge that they refer to an instructional book specifically addressing the required technique.

Foreword

The projects in this book were painted by Plaid's most respected and best-selling artists. Each has developed their own style through years of teaching, demonstrating, and writing.

There is a wide range of surfaces used in this book—wood, paper, ceramics, and metal. Plaid has developed a paint for every need. For wood, metal, terra-cotta, and canvas surfaces, acrylic colors and artists' pigments are the paint of choice. When painting on glass and ceramics, enamels should be used for ease of application and ultimate durability—these paints are top-rack dishwasher safe. With painting on paper so popular because of the scrapbooking trend, papier paint is the one to use.

Table of Contents

General Instructions—Supplies

Brushes

Decorative painting uses "artist brushes" made of natural hairs or high-quality synthetic hairs. Brush quality is important to successfully achieve a painted design, so shop for the best you can afford. The size of the brush to use depends on the size of the area to be painted.

Flat, round, and liner are the most important brushes. You can do all your decorative painting with these three brushes alone. However, as with most hobbies and crafts, as you become more proficient, you find yourself requiring more refined tools.

Angulars—are flat brushes with bristles cut at an angle. They are used to paint fine chiseled edges, curved strokes, and to blend.

Filberts—are flat brushes with a rounded tip that can make fine chiseled lines. They are also helpful for curving stripes, filling in, and blending.

Flats—are brushes with flattened ferrules, rectangular in shape, with long bristles. The chiseled edge makes fine lines while the flat edge makes wide strokes. They can carry a large quantity of paint without having to reload often. Flats can be used for base-coating, double-loading, floating, and washing.

Liners—are round, thin brushes used to paint small areas. Scrollers and script liners have longer bristles. They are used to paint fine lines and calligraphic strokes. Detail work, such as out-lining, facial features, tendrils, veins in leaves and flowers, etc., is done with these brushes.

Mops—are round brushes with soft long bristles. They are used for smoothing, softening, and blending edges.

Filberts

Flats

Washes

Short Flats

Rounds

Rounds

Liners

Rounds—have a round ferrule and the bristles taper to a fine point at the tip. These brushes are used for base-coating and are helpful with strokework. The fine tip works well for painting details and tiny spaces.

Scruffy Brushes—are rectangular brushes with short bristles. They can be purchased or you can simply use a damaged or worn-out flat brush. They cannot be used for strokes, but work well for pouncing, stippling, dry-brushing, or dabbing.

Sponge Brushes—are used when evenly applying base coats on project surfaces before decorative painting is applied. Sponge or foam, brushes are also used for finishing.

Sponge Rollers—are specifically designed paint rollers with tapered ends to prevent paint ridges. Sponge, or foam, rollers are ideal for achieving a quick background.

Stencil Brushes—are round brushes with either soft or stiff bristles. These brushes need very little paint loaded onto them. Excess paint is dabbed off onto a paper towel before applying it to project surface. Paint is applied to project either with a pouncing motion or a circular motion.

Wash Brushes—are large flat brushes used for base-coating, washing, and finishing.

Fan

Angular

Scruffy

Stencil

Sponge Brush

Sponge Roller

Brush Care & Cleanup

Brushes must be properly cleaned and cared for. A new, quality brush has sizing in it to hold the bristles in place. Before painting, remove sizing by gently rolling bristles between your fingers. Then thoroughly clean brush with water.

After painting is complete, wash brush, being careful not to abuse bristles. Work bristles back and forth in a brush cleaner. Once paint is removed, leave cleaner in bristles and shape them with your fingers. Rinse brush again before painting.

Soft Cloth—is used for wiping brushes. Paper towels can damage bristles.

Water Container—is used with clean water for rinsing brushes and provides a surface to rest brushes, keeping ferrules and handles out of water.

Paints

Paints are the most important supply when painting. Consider the surface you are painting when choosing your paint.

Acrylic Colors—are richly pigmented paints that have been formulated for design painting purposes. They are ready to use with no mixing required. While there are many subtle pre-mixed shades, there are also pure, intense, universal pigment colors that are true to the nature of standard pigments. These paints can be used on almost any type of surface.

Artists' Pigment Colors—are concentrated pigmentation color to give a higher coverage and mixability.

Enamels—are water-based, non-toxic, and dry to an opaque finish and gloss sheen. Glass and ceramic pieces painted with enamels can be hand-washed and are top-rack dishwasher safe. Do not paint within ⅛" of top rim of glasses or mugs or use in direct contact with food. Reverse-painting on the backs of clear glass plates is recommended if plates are to be used with food.

Indoor/Outdoor Acrylic Craft Paints—are durable high-gloss enamels. This is the one paint for glass, ceramics, and indoor/outdoor use. These paints are weather resistant, which makes them the best choice for projects that will be used outdoors.

Papier Paints—can be used several ways. You can dilute them to create light watercolor washes, brush them on more heavily for a dimensional look, or simply apply them directly to the surface for a thicker 3-D effect. These paints can be mixed to create fun new colors in addition to the beautiful colors straight from the bottle.

Mediums

Blending Gel—makes blending of paint colors easier. This gel keeps paints moist, giving more time to shade and highlight before the project dries.

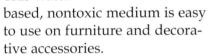

Crackle Medium—achieves what normally takes wind and weather many years. This water-based, nontoxic medium is easy to use on furniture and decorative accessories. When applied over a dry acrylic base coat, it forms cracks instantly.

Enamel Clear Medium—can be used to create floating effects without losing adhesion on the glass. It can be used on glass and glazed ceramics in a similar fashion to floating medium. You can also mix 1:1 with paint to create a transparent paint.

Floating Medium—is used instead of water for floating, shading, or highlighting. It is easier to float a color with medium than water because it allows more control, and the medium will not run like water.

Flow Medium—is the most important feature for painting on paper. It gives the paint a vehicle to flow, mix, and/or move easily over paper without wrinkling and buckling from overwetting with water.

Glazing Medium—when mixed with acrylic paint, gives the perfect consistency to a topcoat that can be textured with other techniques. It can also be used as an antiquing medium.

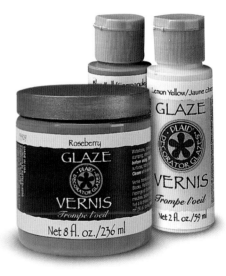

Miscellaneous Supplies

Art Eraser — to remove stray lines

Blow Dryer — to speed drying

Extender — to slow drying

Multipurpose Sealer — to prepare surface before painting

Palette — to arrange and mix paints as well as to load and blend paints into brushes

Palette Knife — to mix paints

Paper Towels — to clean up

Ruler — to measure placement

Sanding Ovals — to remove rough spots from surfaces

Sandpaper — to remove rough spots from painting surfaces

Satin Exterior Varnish — to protect projects

Sea Sponge — to sponge-paint

Tack Cloth — to remove dust after sanding

Waxed Palette — to arrange and mix paints as well as to load and blend paints into brushes

Wood Filler — to fill holes and gaps in wood

Wood Sealer — to prepare wooden surface before painting

Note: See individual project instructions for additional supplies needed.

Transfer Tools

Low-tack Masking Tape — to secure patterns

Pencil — to trace patterns from the book or to transfer a pattern onto a prepared surface. A soft-leaded #2 pencil works best.

Permanent Marker — to trace patterns

Photocopier & Paper — to enlarge and copy patterns from book before transferring onto painting surface

Stylus — to transfer a photocopied or traced design onto a prepared surface. A pencil or a ballpoint pen with no ink may also be used.

Tracing Paper — to trace patterns from the book. Choose a tracing paper that is as transparent as possible for intricate designs.

Transfer Paper — to transfer a traced or photocopied pattern onto the project surface. Choose transfer paper that has a water-soluble coating in a color that will be visible on the base-coat color of the project surface.

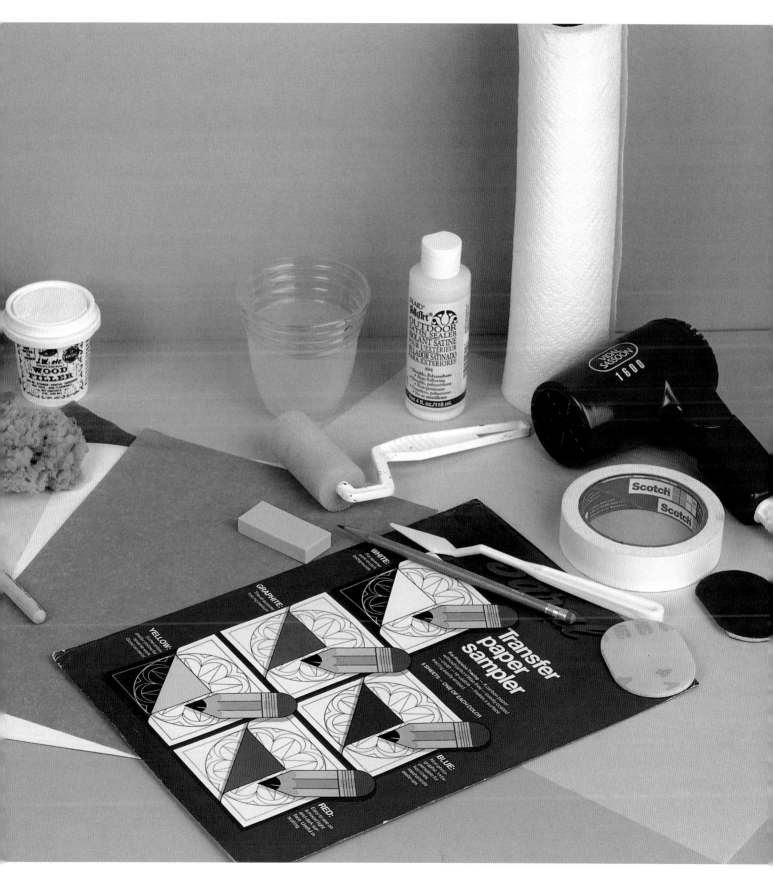

Finishes

Erase remaining pattern lines. Use a high-quality varnish or sealer. Choose sealers that are nonyellowing and quick-drying. Using a tack cloth, remove lint, dust, or dirt before applying a finish.

If project is new wood and was stained or glazed, wood will soak up most of the first coat of finish, requiring more coats than a painted surface. If project is to be used outdoors or receive heavy traffic, apply a protective sealer such as polyurethane. Waterproof exterior acrylics need not be varnished.

Acrylic Sealer—is brushed on to protect projects after paint is dry. Apply 2–3 coats.

Aerosol Finish—is sprayed onto surfaces to seal and protect against moisture, soil, and dust. Spray dry project with sealer. Spray several times to provide smooth finish. Let dry between coats. Sand surface with wet 400-grit sandpaper or with a fine-grade steel wool. Tack away dust.

Artists' Varnish—protects, seals, and offers resistance from scratches and water spotting. Apply this brush-on water-based finish with a sponge brush after paint has dried.

Dry & Cure

After applying paints to glass surfaces, allow paints to cure for 21 days before using—OR—bake. To bake, let paint dry one hour, then place projects in a cool oven. Heat oven to 350°F and bake for 30 minutes. Allow oven to cool with project in it.

General Instructions—Prepare

Preparing Surfaces

Before beginning a project, read through the instructions. Follow the steps in order. Prepare the project surface with primer or base coat before applying patterns and paint. Projects painted without primer can peel, crack, or powder off. Avoid touching areas to be painted, as skin oil can harm paint's adhesion.

When sanding between coats of primer, paint, or varnish, check surface for smoothness.

If surface appears to be scratched after sanding, you are either using sandpaper that is too coarse or sanding before product is dry. If this happens, let the surface dry and sand again. Use a tack cloth to wipe away dust after each sanding.

Glass & Ceramic

Use rubbing alcohol to clean a glass surface. Apply a glass-and-tile medium to these nonporous surfaces to give the project some "tooth" for the paint to hold onto.

Metal

An enamel is the best type of paint to use on metal to ensure that the design will not peel off. Tin has long been used for painting (also called "tole" painting), and features items such as watering cans, buckets, kitchen scoops, and garden tools. Today, even rusted tin is popular. Wrought iron also has become more popular with greater interest in yard and garden decor.

New Tin

Some new tins may need no preparation. However, galvanized tin has an oily film that must be removed before painting. Using a sponge or soft cloth, clean the item with a solution of water and vinegar. Do not immerse the piece in water as water can be trapped in tight areas of the piece, causing problems later. Rinse well and dry thoroughly. Painted or enameled tin requires damp-sponging with water, then drying.

Old Metal

Sand the surface or rub with steel wool to remove loose paint or rust and to smooth imperfections. Wipe well with a cloth dampened in turpentine. Let dry. Apply a metal primer. Let primer dry thoroughly, then sand lightly with fine-grade sandpaper. Wipe with a tack cloth.

Wood

Be certain the surface is clean and free from dirt and oil. Sand new wood with 120-grit sandpaper until surface appears smooth, then use 220-grit sandpaper to finish. Sand with the grain of the wood.

If wood is to be painted with a light color over an already dark finish, first apply a coat of white spray primer. The primer seals the wood and prevents any knotholes from bleeding through. After primer is dry, sand surface with 220-grit sandpaper, working with the grain of the wood. Wipe away dust.

Fill nail holes, cracks, or gaps where sections of wood meet, with a neutral color of stainable filler. Using a palette knife, apply as little as possible to fill area. Remove excess while wet. Let dry, then sand smooth. If area appears sunken after drying, repeat to level out. Sand again when dry.

Base-coating

The first coat of paint that is applied to project. When base-coating elements of the design, start applying paint at center of area and work paint to outer edge. When working on very small areas, outline with a liner before filling in. Several thin coats are better that one or two thick ones.

Masking-off an Area

With ruler and pencil, mark lines for tape to run against. Apply tape smooth along the lines. Be certain to securely press down tape edges to prevent paint from seeping underneath. Paint untaped areas (do not worry about paint overlapping tape.) remove tape before paint is dry.

Transferring Patterns

Project patterns are included in this book. To keep these pages intact, photocopy them, enlarging or reducing as necessary to fit surface.

Another transferring option is to place tracing paper over the pattern in the book. Secure with low-tack masking tape. Using a pencil, trace the major design elements onto tracing paper. Use the detailed pattern and the photograph as guides when painting.

To transfer, position traced or photocopied pattern on project, securing one side with masking tape. Slip transfer paper between pattern and project surface. Make certain that the velvet coating is against the base-coated surface. Using a stylus, retrace pattern lines with enough pressure to transfer the lines but not so much as to indent the surface. Use dark transfer paper for light surfaces and light (white) transfer paper for dark surfaces.

Another transferring option would be to use chalk. Rub chalk across the back of the pattern, place on prepared surface, and retrace the pattern lines with a stylus.

When using a pattern, first transfer only the main outline of the design onto the project to be base-coated. After the base-coating is dry, transfer the pattern details onto the design for painting, shading, and highlighting.

Painting Tips

- Read through instructions before beginning a project. Paint the project steps in the order specified. Keep the instructions and project photograph handy while working.
- Try a few practice strokes before painting the design.
- Squeeze paint onto palette, making a puddle of paint about the size of a nickel.
- Pull color with brush from edge of puddle. Avoid dipping brush in center of puddle, putting too much paint on the brush.
- Let each coat dry before applying another. If area is cool to the touch, it is most likely still wet.
- Acrylic paints blend easily. Add white to lighten a color; add black to darken a color.

Painting Terms

Accent: The addition of a contrasting or complementary color related to other colors in the composition. Accents help add interest and tie design elements together.

Anchor: To float a dark shading color, shadow, or highlight over an undercoated subject. The anchor is allowed to dry completely, and then the painting technique is applied over the top. This technique is usually used with acrylics. Because of the transparency of acrylics, often shadows move around too much when blended. By applying an anchor before blending begins, this problem is avoided.

Brush-mix: Mixing two or more colors together on a palette with a brush rather than a palette knife. Simply pull a small amount from each color listed with a "plus" and blend lightly with brush. Each time you brush-mix, the color may be slightly different, which adds variety.

Consistency: The thickness or thinness of a paint. You need different consistencies for different techniques. To blend, paint must be thicker. To stroke, paint must be thinner. To paint line-work, paint must be the consistency of ink.

Contrast: The sharp difference between two or more colors. When two colors meet, one edge must be light (usually the edge toward the front of the design) and the other edge must be dark (usually the edge toward the back).

Cure: Curing is more than just drying. Paint may appear dry on the surface yet not be dry underneath the surface. The curing time depends on paint, thickness, types of extenders used, room temperature, air circulation, and humidity. Most instructions give a maximum amount of time to be certain paint is cured.

Dirty Brush: When shading and blending, or adding foundation, a color change may be needed. It is not always necessary to wash the brush between colors. You may dry-wipe the brush (leaving it "dirty") and pick up another color.

Glaze: By applying a transparent layer of color to an area, glazing strengthens highlights or shadows, or adds slight tints of color. Paint is thinned with blending gel to make paint transparent. This "glaze" is then pulled over an area to tone a color or add more darkness to a shaded area.

Inky: Mix paint with water until paint is consistency of ink.

Outline: Use a #1 liner or the very fine point of any good brush. Load the brush with inky paint.

Side-load: Fill a flat or angled brush with extender or floating medium. Dab on paper towel. Load one side of brush with paint color. Do not allow paint to travel more than one-fourth of the way across the brush. Blend brush on wet palette.

Spatter: Fill a toothbrush or stencil brush with thinned paint. Pull a palette knife toward you across bristles to splatter specks of paint onto the surface.

Stipple: Pounce tips of brush bristles on project surface. Wipe brush with a rag to clean. Do not wash brush until finished. You cannot stipple with a damp brush.

Thin: Dilute paint with water, extender, or glazing medium as instructions require.

Tint: Load a small amount of contrasting paint on a filbert brush and apply to project. To soften color, lightly brush with mop brush.

Wet-on-wet: While paint is still wet, pick up shading or highlighting color on brush and paint area, blending new color into previous one.

General Instructions—Paint the Design

Loading a Flat or Filbert Brush

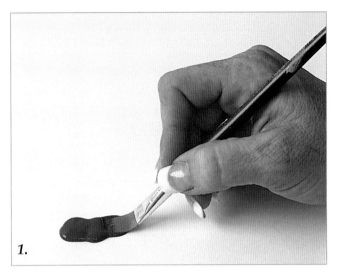

1. Squeeze a small puddle of paint onto palette. Place brush at edge of puddle. Pull paint out from edge of puddle with brush, loading one side of brush.

2. Flip brush over and repeat to load other side. Continue flipping brush and brushing back and forth on palette to fully load bristles.

Loading a Liner or Scroller

1. Squeeze a small puddle of paint onto palette and dilute it at one edge with water. Thin paint to an "inky" consistency so that it flows.

2. Pull liner along diluted edge of puddle, loading paint into bristles. Twirl bristles at edge of puddle to sharpen point.

Loading a Round Brush

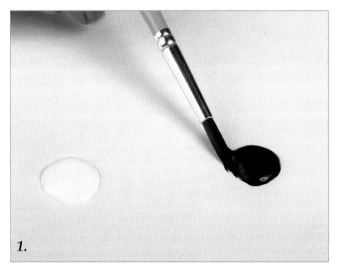

1. Squeeze a small puddle of paint onto palette. Hold brush at edge of puddle. Push brush straight down into puddle.

Loading a Scruffy Brush

1. Squeeze a small puddle of paint onto palette. Hold brush at edge of puddle. Push brush straight down. Rotate brush. Be certain bristles are loaded.

Double-loading a Flat Brush

1. Touch one side of brush into paint color. Touch opposite side into another color. Paint will be definitely separated on brush.

2. Stroke brush to blend colors at brush center. Colors should remain unblended on corners and form a middle value in the center.

19

Using a Painting Worksheet

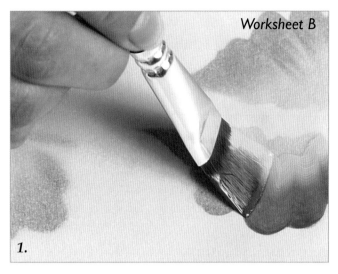

Worksheet A

Painting worksheets demonstrate a variety of painting techniques and allow you to practice a stroke before attempting it on a project surface.

Some worksheets can be purchased with a protective plastic coating so you can paint directly on it, then wipe it clean when finished. The worksheets in this book can be used similarly. Color-copy the worksheet from the project you will be working on, then cover it with clear plastic wrap, or a sheet of acetate.

Arrows may be added to a worksheet example to show the direction in which a stroke should be done as shown in Worksheet A. Apply strokes following the direction of the arrows, painting petals first, then center, then details.

Some worksheets group design elements together. Using the worksheet examples, simply follow the succession in numerical order where given as shown in Worksheet B.

Still other worksheets have step-by-step instructions as shown in Worksheet C on page 21. Whatever the style, worksheets are provided to assist the artist. The paint colors to be used are not listed on the painting worksheets, as paint names change. Refer to the project instructions for the brush type and paint color to be used.

Once you feel confidant with your painting ability, feel free to mix and match techniques and patterns from a combination of worksheets. For example, create a garden scene of your own by using the Dragonfly and Bee examples on page 29, the Iris on page 35, the Bird on page 71, and Butterfly from page 73. Let your imagination guide your design.

2.

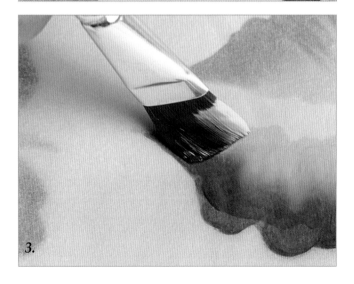

3.

Basic Brush Strokes Worksheet

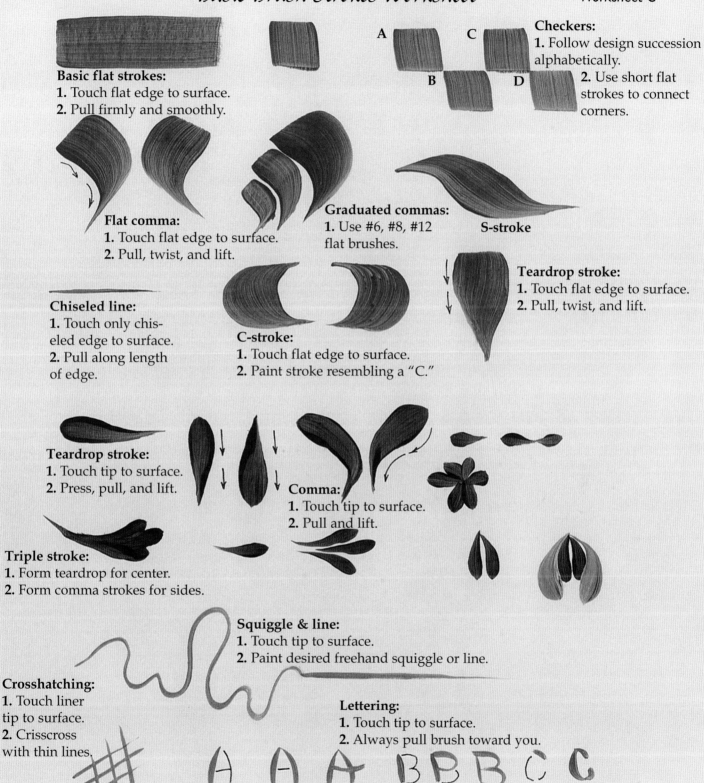

Basic flat strokes:
1. Touch flat edge to surface.
2. Pull firmly and smoothly.

Checkers:
1. Follow design succession alphabetically.
2. Use short flat strokes to connect corners.

A C
B D

Flat comma:
1. Touch flat edge to surface.
2. Pull, twist, and lift.

Graduated commas:
1. Use #6, #8, #12 flat brushes.

S-stroke

Chiseled line:
1. Touch only chiseled edge to surface.
2. Pull along length of edge.

C-stroke:
1. Touch flat edge to surface.
2. Paint stroke resembling a "C."

Teardrop stroke:
1. Touch flat edge to surface.
2. Pull, twist, and lift.

Teardrop stroke:
1. Touch tip to surface.
2. Press, pull, and lift.

Comma:
1. Touch tip to surface.
2. Pull and lift.

Triple stroke:
1. Form teardrop for center.
2. Form comma strokes for sides.

Squiggle & line:
1. Touch tip to surface.
2. Paint desired freehand squiggle or line.

Crosshatching:
1. Touch liner tip to surface.
2. Crisscross with thin lines.

Lettering:
1. Touch tip to surface.
2. Always pull brush toward you.

A A A B B B C C

21

Antiquing

1. Brush antiquing medium over surface and wipe away excess with a soft cloth. *Note: Antiquing glaze can be made by mixing acrylic paint color with glazing medium (1:3). Apply as with antiquing medium.*

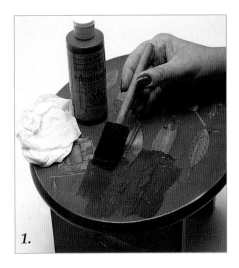

2. Using a soft towel, wipe off excess antiquing medium. Keep the medium evenly spread on the project. Let project completely dry. *Note: If a darker color is desired, repeat the antiquing process.*

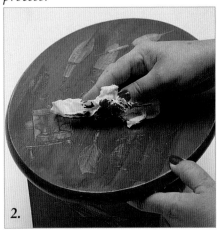

Using a Chiseled Edge

1. Fully load a flat with paint to avoid running out while pulling along line. Keeping brush perpendicular to surface, pull along length of chiseled edge. Load brush as needed and continue pulling smooth even strokes to keep lines consistent.

Crackling

1. Base-coat project with acrylic paint. Let dry. Using sponge brush, apply a generous coat of crackle medium. Let dry. Apply an acrylic topcoat. As it dries, cracks will form. *Note: A thick topcoat produces large cracks. A thin topcoat produces smaller cracks.*

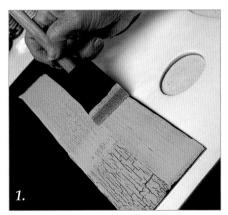

Distressing

1. Base-coat the surface with desired paint color. Let dry. Using a wax stick, apply steaks of wax to areas of finish where a worn-paint look is desired.

2. Apply topcoat of paint in different color to completely cover the first color. Let dry. Sand through top in the area where wax was applied to reveal some of the bottom layer.

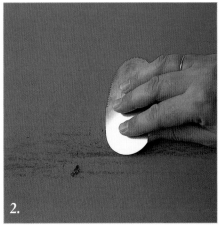

Dry-brushing

1. Load flat, scruffy, or stencil brush with paint color on palette. Blend paint into brush in a circular motion by rubbing it into a paper towel. Only a hint of paint should remain in brush.

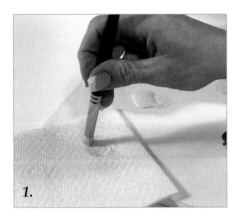

2. Swirl brush on painting surface while applying pressure to either shade or highlight, adding just a touch of color. The result should be a soft-shaded look.

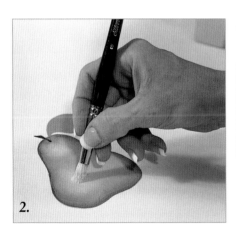

Floating

1. Side-load a flat brush with floating medium. Blot excess on paper towel.

2. Apply a thin layer of floating medium to surface.

3. Load one corner of brush with paint. Gently stroke brush on a palette, turn brush over and blend on other side.

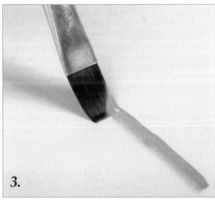

4. Soften, until you have a smooth gradation of color to clear floating medium.

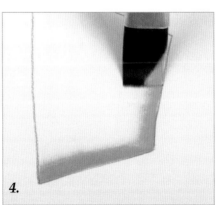

Shading & Highlighting

Shading:

1. Using a side-loaded brush, apply dark paint on slightly moistened surface.

Highlighting:

1. Using a side-loaded brush, apply light paint on slightly moistened surface.

Shimmering

1. With a side-loaded flat brush that has been softened on palette, float color where shimmer is desired.

Quickly flip brush over and float color against the color that was just placed. *Note: This will make a shimmer effect with outside (on both sides) fading out, leaving center of shimmer the brightest.*

Sponging

1. Dip a damp sponge into paint on a palette. Blot on a paper towel to remove excess. Press sponge on the base-painted project, then lift. Repeat, turning sponge a bit each time.

Stenciling

1. Using a dry stencil brush for each color, dip bristle tips into paint color on palette. Brush paint on paper towel to remove almost all paint.

2. Apply paint in cut-out areas of stencil. Gradually build up color to desired intensity. Do not rinse brushes until stenciling is completed.

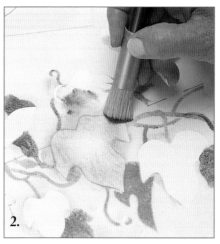

Washing

1. On palette, mix paint with water (1:4) or with glazing medium for a thinned transparent "wash."

2. Load brush with wash and use long smooth strokes for an even coverage.

Notes: The background color should slightly show through wash.

This technique will create a watercolor effect.

Birdhouses in the Garden Cigar-box Purse
by Donna Dewberry

Gather These Supplies

Painting Surface:
- Wooden cigar box, 8½" x 8" x 2"

Acrylic Paint Colors:
- Butter Pecan
- Fresh Foliage
- Linen
- Purple Passion
- Thicket
- Violet Pansy
- Wicker White

Artist's Pigment Color:
- Burnt Umber 28

Medium & Finish:
- Floating
- Spray lacquer, gloss

Brushes:
- Filberts: #6, #8
- Flats: #6, #8, #12, ¾", 1"
- Script liner: #2
- Scruffy

Other Supplies:
- Bag boutique handle
- Drill & drill bits
- Fern stencil
- Masking tape
- Palette
- Pencil
- Ruler
- Sandpaper
- Scissors
- Tack cloth
- Transfer tools

Surface Preparation

Note: Refer to General Instructions on pages 8–24.

1. Sand surface to remove rough areas. Using tack cloth, remove all traces of sanding dust.

2. Using 1" flat, base-coat box with one coat of Butter Pecan. Let dry.

3. Lightly sand surface again to remove any raised wood grain. Apply a second coat of Butter Pecan. Let dry.

4. Position and secure fern stencil on front of cigar box with masking tape. Using scruffy, pounce to fill in stencil with Linen. Let dry.

5. Transfer Birdhouses in the Garden Pattern on page 30 onto cigar box.

Paint the Design

Note: Refer to Birdhouses & Bugs Painting Worksheet on page 29.

Birdhouses:

1. Using 1" flat, paint birdhouse shapes with Linen.

2. Double-load ¾" flat with Burnt Umber and floating medium. Using flat side of brush, add shading on edges of birdhouse shapes.

3. Load ¾" flat with floating medium and Thicket. Blend on palette to create a thin wash. Apply wash below birdhouses for ground base.

4. Double-load #8 flat with Burnt Umber and Wicker White. Add a touch of floating medium and blend well to soften. Using flat side of brush and keeping Burnt Umber to outer edge, paint holes in birdhouses.

5. Using same brush and colors, but staying on chiseled edge and leading with Wicker White, touch, lean, and pull to form birdhouse perches.

6. Pick up fresh paint on #8 flat to paint roof for birdhouse at right. Use same stroke that was used for perches. Overlap rows starting at bottom and working up.

7. Load script liner with inky Burnt Umber. Using tip of brush, pull accent lines from outer edge in, then add a darker line to left side of holes. Turn brush over and dip handle into puddle of Burnt Umber. Dot end of each perch.

8. Load script liner with a touch of Wicker White. Highlight end of perches and inside holes.

9. Double-load scruffy with Thicket and Wicker White. Add a touch of Burnt Umber to Thicket side. Pounce mossy roof for birdhouse at left.

10. Using same brush and colors, add moss around bottoms of both birdhouses.

11. Add a touch of Fresh Foliage to brush and pounce a little on roof.

Continued on page 28.

Grass:

1. Load #12 flat with Thicket, then add a touch of floating medium. Using chisel edge of brush, pull grass from moss upward.

Stalk Flowers:

Note: There are three sizes of stalk flowers.

1. Double-load #8 filbert with Purple Passion and Wicker White. Using flat side of brush, paint the larger of purple stalk flowers at left by starting at top and pulling downward.

2. Double-load #6 flat with Purple Passion and Wicker White. Paint stalk flower in center, starting at bottom and pulling out and up.

3. Load #6 filbert with Violet Pansy, then add a touch of Wicker White and blend well to soften. Using flat side of brush, paint small stalk flower on right.

Leaves:

1. Load #12 flat with floating medium. Dip one corner into Burnt Umber, then blend well on palette, adding more floating medium as needed until color is transparent.

2. Using flat side of brush, paint large brown one-stroke leaves throughout design.

3. Load script liner with inky Thicket. Using tip of brush, add vine, winding around small birdhouse.

4. Load #6 flat with Thicket, then add a touch of floating medium to soften. Paint tiny one-stroke leaves on vine.

Colored Moss:

1. Load scruffy with Wicker White. Pick up a touch of Violet Pansy on one side of brush and Purple Passion on other side.

2. Using a light up-and-down pouncing motion and tilting handle slightly to allow only one side of brush to touch, pounce colored moss hills. Turn brush around and pounce so other color is dominant.

Dragonfly:

1. Load #12 flat with Wicker White, then add a touch of floating medium and blend well. Using flat side of brush, paint two largest wings on dragonfly. Using same brush and chiseled edge, paint two smaller wings.

2. Load #8 flat with Thicket, then side-load a touch of Burnt Umber by stroking next to puddle of paint, allowing tip of bristles of one corner to touch puddle. Paint small segments for body. Use more pressure at head area to make sections larger, then use less pressure near tail.

3. Load script liner with Thicket, then add a touch of Burnt Umber to the tip. Using tip of brush, add two small strokes for split tail and two for the antennae.

4. Outline wings with inky Burnt Umber. Add veining in wings.

5. Using same brush and inky paint, add an accent line to large one-stroke leaves. *Optional: Add a bee or ladybug if you choose.*

Side Borders:

1. Load ¾" flat with Burnt Umber. Work some floating medium into brush to achieve a slightly transparent color. Using flat side of brush, paint wide stripes on box sides.

2. Load script liner with inky Thicket. Paint thin stripes on box sides. Let box dry.

3. Sign your name. Let dry.

Finish

1. Spray with one light coat of lacquer. Let dry. Apply two or three additional coats, allowing ample drying time between coats.

2. Measure where handle will attach and mark lightly with a pencil.

3. Using drill and a bit that is slightly smaller than cord through center of handle, drill hole at each place that was marked.

4. Cut small beads off one end of handle and disconnect wooden support.

5. Thread one end through one predrilled hole, then attach a small bead and tie a knot. Attach remaining side of handle in same manner.

Birdhouses & Bugs Painting Worksheet

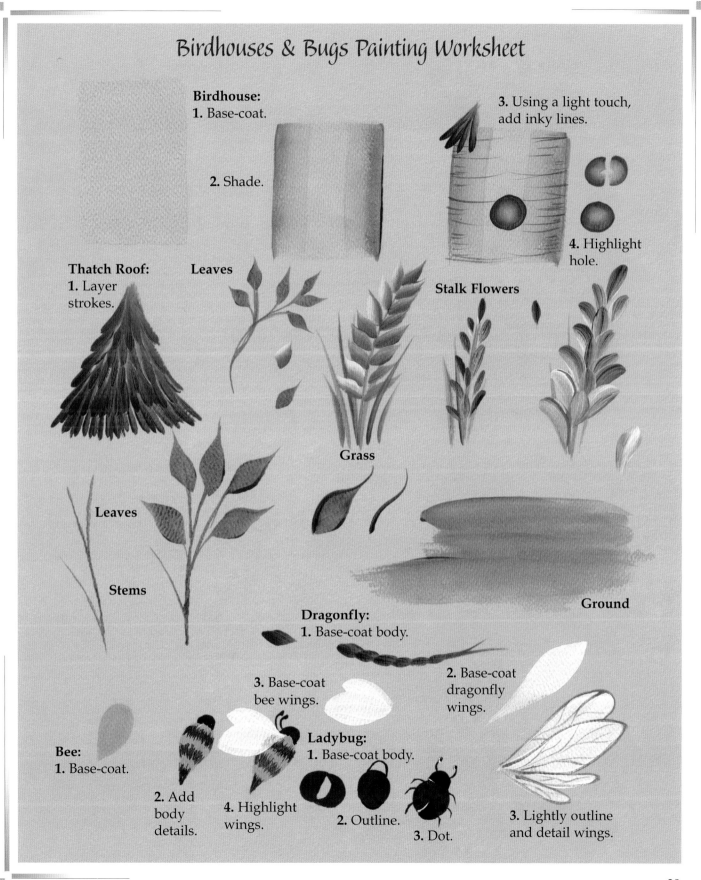

Birdhouse:
1. Base-coat.

2. Shade.

3. Using a light touch, add inky lines.

4. Highlight hole.

Thatch Roof:
1. Layer strokes.

Leaves

Stalk Flowers

Grass

Leaves

Stems

Ground

Dragonfly:
1. Base-coat body.

2. Base-coat dragonfly wings.

3. Base-coat bee wings.

Ladybug:
1. Base-coat body.

Bee:
1. Base-coat.

2. Add body details.

4. Highlight wings.

2. Outline.

3. Dot.

3. Lightly outline and detail wings.

Birdhouses in the Garden Pattern

Pattern is actual size.

Dragonfly & Iris Desk Set
Instructions begin on page 32.

Dragonfly & Iris Desk Set

Telephone Book, Note Box, Pen Holder, Mirror & Lamp

by Di Singleton
Photo shown on page 31.

Gather These Supplies

Painting Surfaces:
- Hardback telephone book, 8" x 7¼"
- Rounded hurricane lamp with wooden base & tulip glass, 3" dia. x 6½" tall
- Wood-framed mirror, frame 10¼" sq.; mirror 4½" sq.
- Wooden notepad holder, 4½" x 7¼" x 2"
- Wooden pen holder, 4¼" x 4" x 3"

Acrylic Paint Colors:
- Autumn Leaves
- Patina
- Settler's Blue
- Silver Sterling (metallic)
- Sunflower

Artists' Pigment Colors:
- Aqua
- Phthalo Green
- Pure Black
- Raw Sienna
- Titanium White
- Turner's Yellow
- Warm White

Enamel Paint Colors:
- Autumn Leaves
- Hunter Green
- Licorice
- Metallic Silver Sterling
- Warm White

Finish:
- Artists' varnish, satin

Brushes:
- Dome round: XS
- Filbert: #6
- Flats: #2, #6
- Liner: 10/0
- Rounds: #3, #5
- Toothbrush
- Wash: 1"

Other Supplies:
- Masking tape
- Palette
- Rubbing alcohol
- Sandpaper
- Soft cloth
- Transfer paper, white
- Transfer tools

Surface Preparation

Note: Refer to General Instructions on pages 8–24.

1. Seal and sand all wooden surfaces and hardback phone book.

2. Clean glass with alcohol.

3. Base-coat all surfaces except glass chimney with a mixture of Settler's Blue plus Aqua (4:1). Let dry.

4. Create a mottled background on each base-coated surface by brushing with Titanium White wash.

5. Using toothbrush, immediately spatter painted surfaces with alcohol. Let dry overnight.

6. Transfer Dragonfly & Iris Patterns on pages 36–37 onto glass. Use white transfer paper or tape traced pattern inside glass.

7. Mix following colors as needed:
- Green mixture: Phthalo Green plus Patina (1:1).
- Enamel Green mixture Hunter Green plus Warm White (1:1). *Note: All other mixtures in instructions are 1:1 ratio unless otherwise stated.*

Paint the Design

Notes: Refer to Dragonfly & Iris Painting Worksheet on page 35.

Paint everything but glass with acrylic colors and artists' pigment colors. Paint glass chimney design with enamels.

Irises:

1. Base-coat flowers and buds with Warm White, then with Sunflower.

2. Shade with side-loaded Turner's Yellow.

3. Paint linework details with Turner's Yellow.

4. Deepen shading with Raw Sienna.

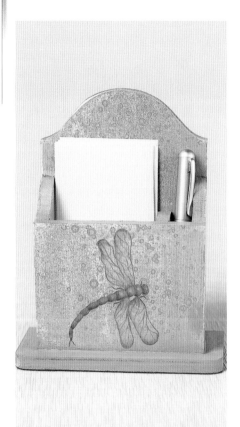

5. Dry-brush highlights with Warm White.

6. Stipple center lines with Raw Sienna, then with Warm White.

7. Add tints of thinned Autumn Leaves.

Dragonflies:

1. Base-coat body with green mixture.

2. Side-load with Phthalo Green and shade behind each segment of each body.

3. Dry-brush highlights with Warm White.

4. Shade around lower edges of wings with side-loaded Phthalo Green.

5. Paint linework legs and veins on wings with a mixture of Pure Black plus Titanium White.

6. Tint next to body with side-loaded Autumn Leaves.

7. Wash wings with transparent Silver Sterling.

Dragonfly on Glass Chimney:

1. Base-coat body with enamel green mixture.

2. Side-load with Hunter Green enamel and shade behind each segment of each body.

3. Dry-brush highlights with Warm White enamel.

4. Shade around lower edges of wings with side-loaded enamel green mixture.

5. Paint linework legs and veins on wings with a mixture of Licorice plus Warm White enamels.

6. Tint next to body with side-loaded Autumn Leaves enamel.

7. Wash wings with transparent Metallic Silver Sterling enamel.

Continued on page 34.

Iris Leaves:

1. Base-coat with green mixture.

2. Shade behind folds, inside of leaves, and   calyxes with Phthalo Green.

3. Dry-brush highlights with green mixture plus Warm White.

Finishing Details:

1. Using wash brush side-loaded with green mixture, deepen color around edges of phone book and mirror frame.

2. Base-coat spine of book with Silver Sterling.

3. Using small flat, paint lettering on phone book with green mixture.

4. Shade letters with Phthalo Green. Highlight letters with dry-brushed Warm White.

5. Sign your name. Let dry for 24 hours.

Finish

1. Finish all pieces except glass chimney with several coats of satin varnish.

2. *Note: Refer to Dry & Cure on page 14.* Let glass chimney dry and cure.

Dragonfly & Iris Painting Worksheet

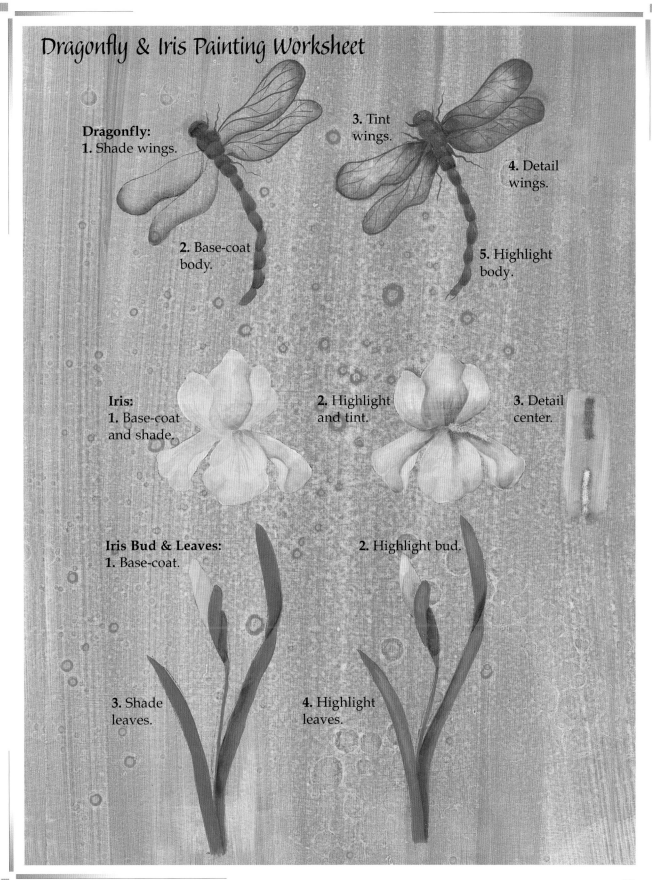

Dragonfly:
1. Shade wings.

2. Base-coat body.

3. Tint wings.

4. Detail wings.

5. Highlight body.

Iris:
1. Base-coat and shade.

2. Highlight and tint.

3. Detail center.

Iris Bud & Leaves:
1. Base-coat.

2. Highlight bud.

3. Shade leaves.

4. Highlight leaves.

Dragonfly & Iris Patterns

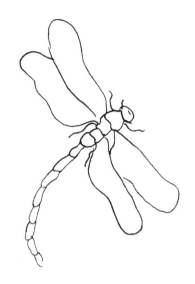

Enlarge patterns 135%.

Dragonfly & Iris Patterns

Enlarge patterns 135%.

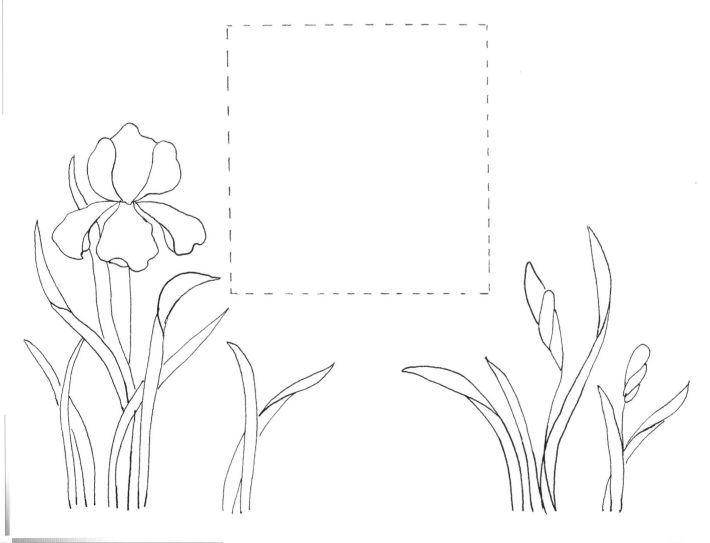

Grapevines Cabinet

by Peggy Boyd

Gather These Supplies

Painting Surface:
- Jelly cabinet, 31" x 55" x 14"

Acrylic Paint Colors:
- Licorice
- Olive Green
- Purple
- Vintage White
- Wicker White

Artists' Pigment Colors:
- Alizarin Crimson
- Burnt Umber
- Green Umber
- Hauser Green Light
- Yellow Ochre

Mediums & Finish:
- Artists' varnish
- Floating
- Glazing
- Wash

Brushes:
- Flats: #8, #10, #12, ¾", 1", 1½"
- Liners: #1, #2
- Old toothbrush
- Round: #6
- Scruffy

Other Supplies:
- Hand tools as needed
- Palette
- Sandpaper, finest finishing grit
- Tack cloth
- Transfer tools

Surface Preparation

Note: Refer to General Instructions on pages 8–24.

1. Remove doors and hardware.

2. Mix a base coat of Licorice, Purple, and wash medium (1:4:5).

3. Test wash on underside of project. Let dry. *Note: If color is too light, add a second coat or add a little more Licorice to the purple glaze mixture.*

4. Base-coat jelly cabinet with mixture. Let dry.

5. Transfer Grapes Pattern on page 41 onto cabinet.

Paint the Design

Note: Refer to Grapevine Painting Worksheet on page 42 and Grape Leaf Painting Worksheet on page 43.
Paint vine, branches, and background leaves first, then grapes, then foreground leaves. This will give appearance of depth as foreground grapes and leaves overlap.

Grapevine:

1. Work floating medium into #10 flat. Double-load with Burnt Umber and Vintage White. Paint vine, following in direction of growth.

2. Fill in with a braided effect.

3. To paint branches, pull brush away from main vine while turning to make stroke taper.

Leaves:

Note: Use a ¾" or 1" flat for larger leaves and a #12 or #10 flat for smaller leaves.

1. Work floating medium into a flat. Load with Olive Green, filling three-fourths of width of brush, then tip other corner with Vintage White.

2. Fill in leaves, following direction of growth. Pull flat from center out, leaving some base coat showing through to give effect of shadow.

3. Before highlighting leaves, establish direction of light. Double-load brush with Olive Green and Vintage White. Repeat fill-in strokes over lighted side of leaves.

4. Fill brush with floating medium. Dip corner of brush into Wicker White. Work paint gently into brush. Stroke with white corner to top or outward on leaf edge. Edge leaf on highlighted side first, creating a sawtooth effect with sharp, straight strokes, pulling down with chiseled-edge of brush. Keep white edge to outside of leaf, lift and repeat all the way around leaf.

Continued on page 40.

5. Make a glaze for shadow side, mixing Green Umber, Hauser Green Light, and glazing medium (1:1:1). Add gradually to white on brush. *Note: This blends colors naturally around edge of leaf.* Follow direction of growth, so strokes should taper toward tips.

6. Load brush with floating medium and tip edge with Wicker White to paint center vein of leaf. Starting at stem end of leaf, pull downward with white edge following, all the way to tip of leaf. *Note: This should be a soft translucent line that curves slightly with the leaf.*

7. If leaf is curved, float a soft highlight of Wicker White across arch of bend.

8. Paint side veins in same way, but lift brush just before edge of leaf, to avoid a blunt end. Apply more floating medium to brush to "erase" a translucent line through the leaf. Follow direction of growth. Let dry.

9. Load a #12 flat with glazing medium and Yellow Ochre, working paint to a translucent pale color on the palette. Brush against grain of leaf, crossing over vein; work in patches on each side to add sunshine.

Turned Leaf:

1. If part of a leaf is turned upward, paint it a lighter or darker shade than main body of leaf, depending on whether it is highlighted or shadowed. Use a smaller flat and create sawtooth edge as other leaves.

Shadow Leaves:

Note: The shadow leaf is a suggestion of foliage around main clusters of grapes and leaves.

1. Make a glaze, mixing Green Umber, Hauser Green Light, and glazing medium (1:1:1). Dip ¾" flat into glaze. Tip highlight side with Wicker White. Work Wicker White into brush by stroking back and forth on palette. *Note: These leaves should be translucent.*

2. Using chiseled edge, angle slightly with shape of leaf, white side upward. Start at back edge of leaf, continually pressing, and move up and down along shape of leaf for a sawtooth appearance as before, returning lower edge of brush to same point. *Note: This forms an accordion-fan shape, with higher strokes in the middle, then tapering smaller toward tip.* Finish by quickly lifting to a sharp tip.

3. Drop down slightly on top of same leaf; repeat movement over top of already painted leaf. A partially unfolded leaf will appear.

4. Use same process to create open leaves. Follow shape of open leaf, using sawtooth movement on one side, then other.

5. Using a #10 or #12 flat, paint smaller leaves along vine.

Grapes Pattern

Enlarge pattern 300%.

Grapes:

Note: For large grapes, use ¾" flat; for smaller grapes, use #12 flat.

1. Fill in grape spheres with Alizarin Crimson. Use a C-stroke to paint half, then a reverse C-stroke on remaining half.

2. Using a C-stroke, highlight one side of grape with Yellow Ochre double-loaded with Alizarin Crimson. Keep Yellow Ochre to lighted side.

3. Make a glaze for grape shadows, mixing Green Umber, Hauser Green Light, and glazing medium (1:1:1). Brush over centers of grapes in the shadow. *Note: Larger grapes at top should be lighter and stand out more. Smaller ones toward bottom and inside cluster will be in shadows.* Let dry.

4. Using #10 flat, float Wicker White on sunny side of grapes.

5. Follow top curve of sphere in a short arched stroke to create highlights with Wicker White.

6. To intensify shading, float translucent Burnt Umber over inside clusters and lower shadowed grapes. Use same stroke as highlights, but follow shape of lower curve.

Tendrils:

1. Create two pools of inky paint on palette, one with Wicker White and the other Olive Green.

2. Drag #2 liner through Wicker White, then Olive Green. Twist while removing from pool to bring bristles to a sharp point and to remove excess paint.

3. Hold brush upright. Start at top of curly vine and pull down slowly, moving hand in a spiral motion. While creating curl, balance hand with small finger.

4. Paint descending curls of vine randomly over grapes and leaves. Be certain they originate from a natural beginning. Add a little Burnt Umber near stalk to simulate a woodier vine.

Buds:

1. Add teardrop-shaped buds to some vine trailers, in a descending or fanned pattern, depending on where they are located.

2. Load #2 liner with Olive Green. Press with tip of bristles to form round head of bud, then pull back sharply toward vine trailers to make pointed tail of teardrop shape.

3. Sign your name. Let project dry 24 hours.

Finish

1. Sand surface to remove rough areas. Using tack cloth, remove all traces of sanding dust.

2. Seal project with three coats of varnish.

3. Replace doors and hardware.

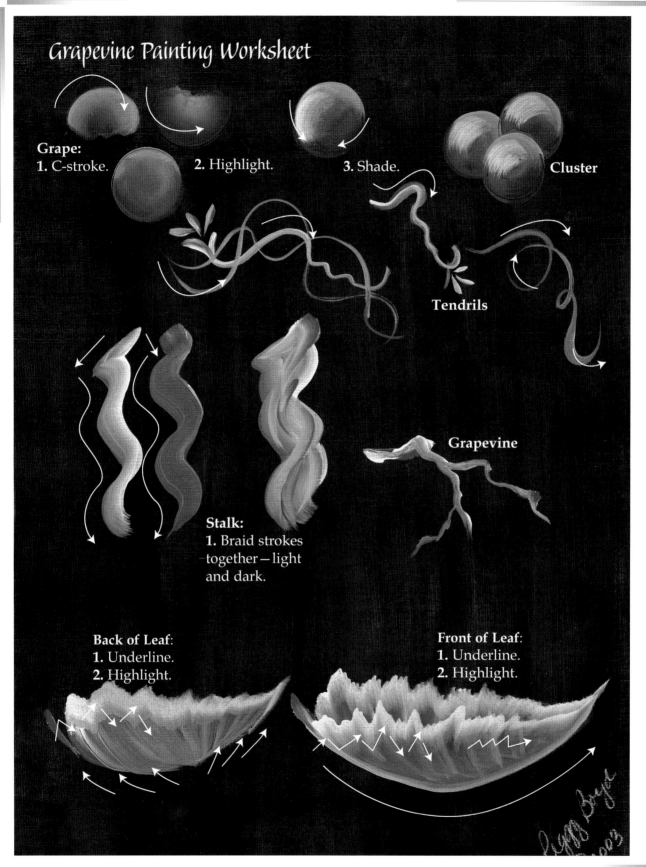

Grapevine Painting Worksheet

Grape:
1. C-stroke.

2. Highlight.

3. Shade.

Cluster

Tendrils

Grapevine

Stalk:
1. Braid strokes together — light and dark.

Back of Leaf:
1. Underline.
2. Highlight.

Front of Leaf:
1. Underline.
2. Highlight.

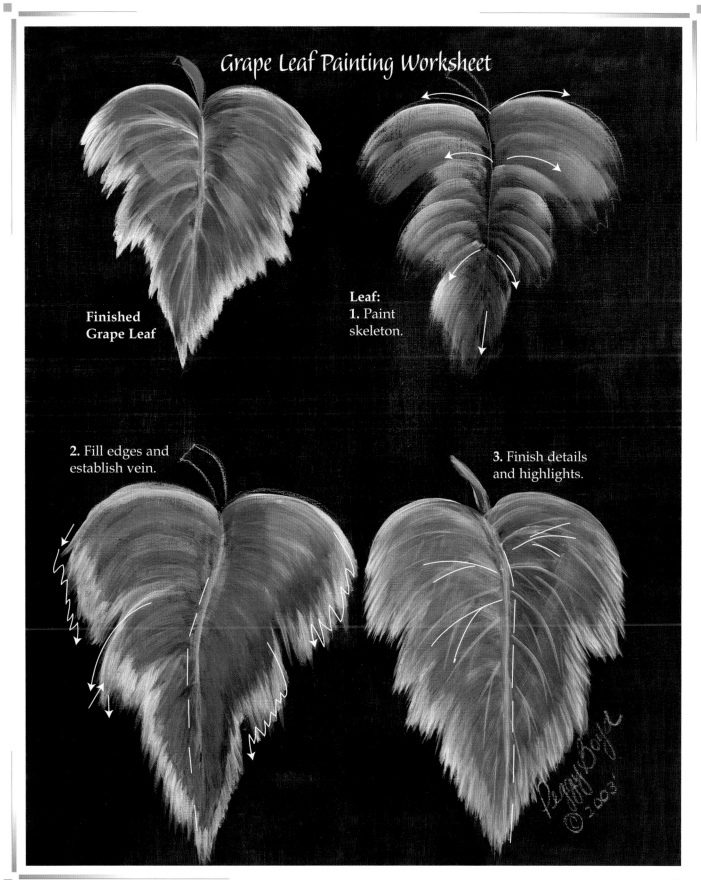

Grape Leaf Painting Worksheet

Finished Grape Leaf

Leaf:
1. Paint skeleton.

2. Fill edges and establish vein.

3. Finish details and highlights.

43

Sunshine Sunflower Footstool

by Priscilla Hauser

Gather These Supplies

Painting Surface:
- Oval wooden stool
  12½" x 7½" x 9"

Acrylic Paint Color:
- Licorice

Artists' Pigment Colors:
- Burnt Sienna
- Burnt Umber
- Green Umber
- Hauser Green Dark
- Medium Yellow
- Pure Orange
- Red Light
- Yellow Light

Mediums & Finish:
- Artists' varnish, satin
- Blending
- Floating

Brushes:
- Flats: #12, #16
- Scruffy

Other Supplies:
- Brown paper bag, without printing
- Palette
- Pencil
- Ruler
- Sandpaper, fine-grit
- Tack cloth
- Transfer tools

Surface Preparation

Note: Refer to General Instructions on pages 8–24.

1. Sand surface to remove rough areas. Using tack cloth, remove all traces of sanding dust.

2. Using pencil, carefully transfer Sunflower Patterns on page 46 (outlines only) onto stool surface. Use a light touch so lines won't be too heavy.

Paint the Design

Notes: Refer to Sunflower Painting Worksheet on page 47.

Paint leaves first, as they are under sunflower.

Leaves:

1. Using #16 flat, anchor shadow with Green Umber. Let dry.

2. Apply blending gel to leaf. Allow 30–60 seconds to penetrate wood.

3. Load #16 flat with Hauser Green Dark. Blend on palette to soften color so it flows from dark to medium to light through brush hairs. Paint this into shadow area of leaves. Carefully scribble color all the way around the leaf.

4. Using #16 flat, apply Green Umber at base of leaf.

5. Wipe brush and blend Green Umber into blending gel, then blend Hauser Green Dark into blending gel. Allow raw wood to be the highlight in the middle.

Sunflower Petals:

Note: Complete blending technique on one petal at a time, painting underneath petals first.

1. Using #12 flat, apply shadows of Burnt Sienna. Let dry.

2. Apply blending gel to petal.

3. Apply more Burnt Sienna to shadow areas.

4. Apply Medium Yellow to remaining area of petal.

5. Wipe brush and blend colors together. Allow background to show through.

6. Using Yellow Light, lighten some petals.

Sunflower Center:

1. Apply blending gel. Allow 30–60 seconds to penetrate wood.

2. Using scruffy, stipple with Burnt Umber, letting it be a bit airy.

3. Highlight with a few dabs of Medium Yellow, Pure Orange, and Red Light. Let dry.

Continued on page 46.

Finishing Details:

1. Mark ½" checkers on stool side. Paint with Licorice.

2. Trim top edge with Licorice.

3. Sign your name. Let dry.

Finish

1. Varnish painted design. Let dry.

2. Rub with paper bag to smooth nap of wood.

3. Apply two or three coats of varnish to entire stool, drying between coats.

Sunflower Patterns

Enlarge patterns 175%.

Sunflower Painting Worksheet

Sunflower:
1. Float petal shadows.

2. Apply blending gel.

3. Apply petal colors.

4. Blend petals.

5. Stipple center.

6. Highlight center.

Leaves:
1. Float shadows.

2. Apply blending gel.

3. Apply colors.

4. Blend.

Tapestry Tassels Lamp

by Karen Embry

Gather These Supplies

Painting Surfaces:
- Lampshade, 4" dia. at top, 12" dia. at bottom x 11" tall
- Wooden lamp base, 5" sq. x 11" tall

Acrylic Paint Colors:
- French Vanilla
- Gray Green
- Nutmeg
- Plum Pudding
- Pure Gold (Metallic)

Artists' Pigment Colors:
- Burnt Carmine
- Burnt Umber

Finish:
- Your choice

Brushes:
- Liners: #2, #4
- Rounds: #2, #4, #6
- Script liners: 2/0, #2
- Stencil: ¾"
- Wash: 1"

Other Supplies:
- Beaded fringe trim
- Gold braided trim, 2 yds.
- Hot-glue gun & glue sticks
- Sandpaper
- Stencil blank material
- Stencil cutter
- Tack cloth
- Transfer tools

Surface Preparation

Note: Refer to General Instructions on pages 8–24.

1. Sand surface to remove rough areas. Using tack cloth, remove all traces of sanding dust.

2. Base-coat lamp base with Gray Green. Let dry.

3. Paint top (indented) edge and bottom edge of lamp base with Pure Gold.

4. Use Tapestry Tassels Lamp Pattern to cut a stencil for checkerboard background.

5. Stencil squares with French Vanilla. Let dry.

6. Transfer the tassel and rope of the Tapestry Tassels Lamp Pattern onto each side of the lamp base.

Continued on page 50.

Tapestry Tassels Lamp Pattern

Enlarge pattern 200%.

Paint the Design

Note: Refer to Tassels Painting Worksheet.

Rope:

1. Base-coat rope with Burnt Umber.

2. Paint second layer slightly inside first layer with Nutmeg.

3. Highlight rope with Pure Gold.

Tassels:

1. Paint tassels with Burnt Carmine.

2. Paint second layer of strings with Plum Pudding.

3. Paint third layer of strings with French Vanilla plus Plum Pudding.

4. Add highlights on right side of each tassel with French Vanilla.

Finish

1. Sign your name. Let dry.

2. Apply finish. Let dry.

3. Attach lamp hardware and electrical cord.

4. Using glue gun, attach beaded trim to lower, inside edge of shade.

5. Glue gold trim to upper and lower edges of lamp base.

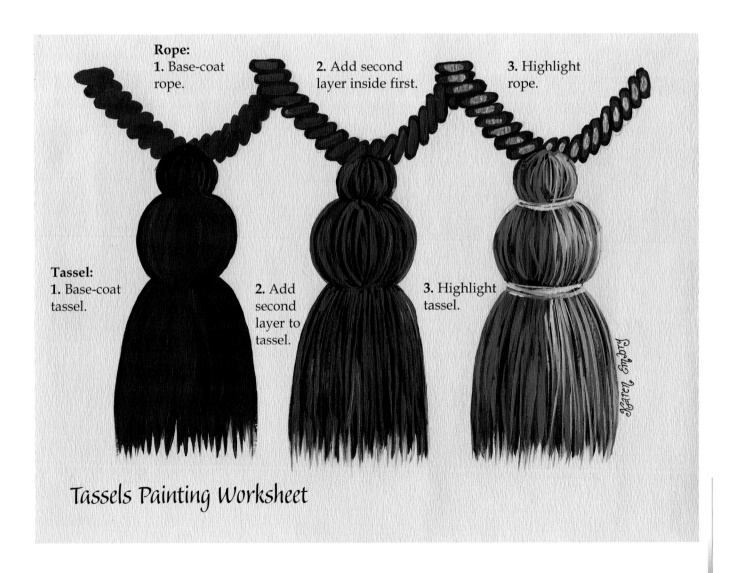

Rope:
1. Base-coat rope.

2. Add second layer inside first.

3. Highlight rope.

Tassel:
1. Base-coat tassel.

2. Add second layer to tassel.

3. Highlight tassel.

Tassels Painting Worksheet

Garden Reflections Mirror Frame

by Gigi Smith-Burns
Photo shown on page 53.

Gather These Supplies

Painting Surface:
- ½"-thick plywood, outside dimensions 8" x 10½"

Acrylic Paint Colors:
- Aspen Green
- Bluebell
- Buttercream
- English Mustard
- Indigo
- Lemonade
- Licorice
- Linen
- Raspberry Wine
- Tangerine
- Wrought Iron

Artists' Pigment Colors:
- Burnt Sienna
- Burnt Umber
- Light Red Oxide
- Warm White

Medium & Finish:
- Blending
- Water-based varnish

Brushes:
- Flats: #2–#10
- Script liner
- Toothbrush

Other Supplies:
- Jigsaw
- Ruler
- Soft cloth
- Transfer tools
- Water-based varnish

Surface Preparation

Note: Refer to General Instructions on pages 8–24.

1. Transfer Garden Reflections Pattern (outline only) on page 52 onto plywood.

2. Using jigsaw, cut out design.

3. Base-coat entire frame with Linen. Let dry.

4. Thin Light Red Oxide with water. Using script liner, make a squiggly line ¼" from outer edge of frame and ¼" from inside edge. Let dry.

5. Lightly transfer Garden Reflections Pattern details onto surface.

Paint the Design

Ribbon:

1. Base-coat ribbon with Light Red Oxide.

2. Shade inside loops, behind knot, outer edge of loops, top and bottom of knot, at twists and turns, and any place ribbon may be coming out from under something with Raspberry Wine.

3. Using shimmer technique, highlight fullest areas of streamers and on top side of loops with a mixture of Light Red Oxide and Warm White.

Leaves:

1. Base-coat leaves with Aspen Green.

2. Shade center vein and base of each leaf with Wrought Iron.

3. Highlight one side of leaf with Tangerine.

4. Reinforce previous shading with Wrought Iron plus a touch of Indigo.

5. Add veins and loosely outline with Wrought Iron.

Black-eyed Susans:

1. Base-coat petals with Lemonade.

2. Shade next to center with English Mustard.

3. Reinforce previous shading with Burnt Sienna.

4. Highlight tips of petals with Buttercream.

5. Add crease lines and loosely outline petals with Burnt Sienna.

6. Base-coat centers with Burnt Sienna. Shade bottom of centers with Burnt Umber plus a bit of Licorice.

7. Add seeds with Licorice.

Filler Flowers:

1. Base-coat petals with Bluebell.

2. Shade next to centers with Indigo. Randomly highlight some petals with Warm White.

3. Using liner handle, dot centers with Tangerine

4. Using #2 flat, stroke in leaves with Aspen Green plus a bit of Wrought Iron.

5. Add center vein and stems with Wrought Iron.

Continued on page 52.

Garden Reflections Pattern

Butterfly:

1. Base-coat wings with wash of Tangerine.

2. Shade next to body with Burnt Sienna.

3. Add details to wings with Licorice.

4. Base-coat body and antennae with Licorice.

5. Add marks on body with Tangerine.

Finishing Details

1. Apply blending gel, then gently shade behind design with Burnt Umber.

2. Add squiggles with Aspen plus Lemonade.

3. Spatter with Burnt Umber.

4. Sign your name. Let dry.

Finish

1. Apply two or more coats of water-based varnish. Let dry.

Enlarge pattern 135%.

Patriotic
Geraniums
Picnic
Basket &
Glasses

Instructions begin on page 56.

Patriotic Geraniums Picnic Basket & Glasses

by Trudy Beard

Photos shown on pages 54–55.

Gather These Supplies

Painting Surfaces:
- Cobalt goblets
- Picnic basket
- Wooden star cutouts

Artists' Pigment Colors:
- Brilliant Ultramarine
- Burnt Carmine
- Hauser Green Dark
- Hauser Green Light
- Napthol Crimson
- Pure Orange
- Titanium White
- Turner's Yellow
- Warm White
- Yellow Citron

Enamel Paint Colors:
- Berry Wine
- Engine Red
- Fresh Foliage
- Green Forest
- Hauser Green Medium
- Metallic Gold
- Pure Orange
- Wicker White

Mediums & Finish:
- Artists' varnish, matte
- Blending
- Enamel clear

Brushes:
- Filbert: #4, #8
- Flat: #6, ½"
- Script liner: #10/0

Other Supplies:
- All-purpose adhesive
- Painter's tape, 2"
- Palette
- Paper towels
- Rubbing alcohol
- Ruler
- Sandpaper: fine-grit, medium-grit
- Stylus
- Tack cloths
- Transfer papers: gray, white
- Transfer tools

Basket Surface Preparation

Note: Refer to General Instructions on pages 8–24.

1. Place painter's tape on diagonal to make stripes. *Note: Do not use regular masking tape.* Continue across, leaving a space at upper right to paint blue and add stars.

2. Remove every-other tape piece. Continue across basket lid until you have 2"-wide spaces in which to paint white stripes.

3. Using ½" flat, paint white stripes with Titanium White. *Note: Two coats may be necessary.* Let dry 5–10 minutes. Remove tape. Let white stripes dry for at least an hour.

4. Place painter's tape on top of white stripe. Paint remaining 2" spaces with ½" flat loaded with two coats Napthol Crimson. Allow red to dry for 5–10 minutes; remove tape. Let all dry for at least an hour.

5. Tape-off outside edge of space left for blue background and painted stars. Paint this area Brilliant Ultramarine. Paint cutout stars with Turner's Yellow.

6. Transfer Patriotic Geraniums Picnic Basket Pattern on page 57 onto basket lid.

Paint the Basket Design

Note: Refer to Geranium Painting Worksheet on page 59.

Leaves & Stems:

1. Load #8 filbert with Hauser Green Dark. Pick up a bit of Hauser Green Light on tip of brush. Fill in leaf shape, starting at outer edge and pulling toward center.

2. Pick up a little Hauser Green Dark, then a bit of Burnt Carmine. Create a center line by applying this dark value in a line down center of leaf. Blend to one side.

3. Highlight by stroking from edge with a small amount of Yellow Citron. Load brush with color, blot, then apply. Strengthen highlight with a mixture of Warm White plus Yellow Citron.

4. Dry-brush touches of accent colors onto each leaf. Accent colors for leaves:
- Napthol Crimson plus Warm White
- Napthol Crimson plus Warm White plus Pure Orange
- Burnt Carmine (in dark areas on leaves)
- Brilliant Ultramarine plus Warm White

Continued on page 58.

Patriotic Geraniums Picnic Basket Pattern

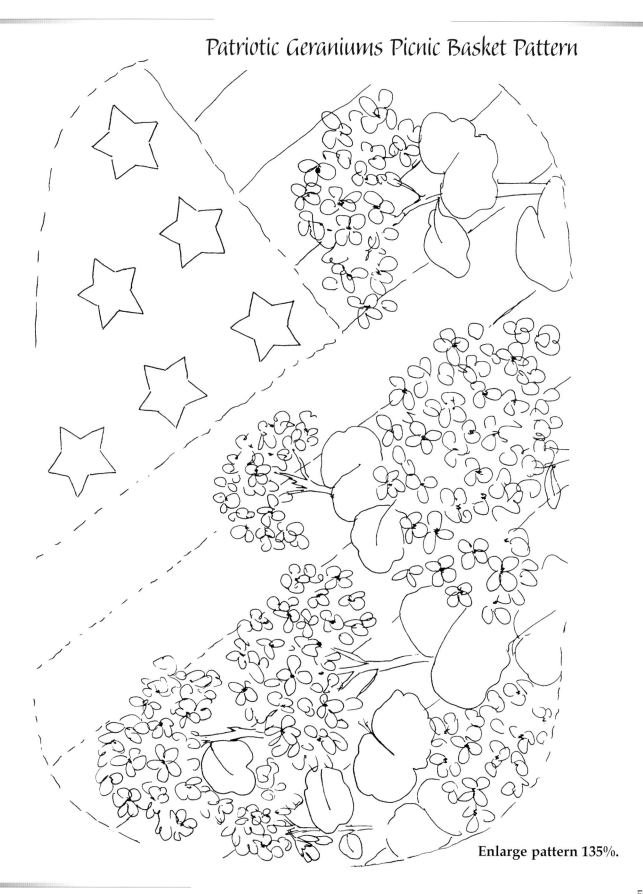

Enlarge pattern 135%.

5. Load script liner with mixture of Warm White plus Yellow Citron that is thinned with water. Paint in a few thin vein lines.

Geraniums:

Note: Paint one geranium at a time so you can work wet-into-wet for a more "painterly" look.

1. Using #8 filbert, block in shape of geranium with a mixture of Burnt Carmine plus Napthol Crimson. *Note: The outer edges are always "ruffled" and have spaces.*

2. Dab or stroke loosely within the shape that you created in Step 1 with Napthol Crimson plus Pure Orange. *Note: Some dark values will show through.*

3. Highlight and create a few defined blossoms with Napthol Crimson plus Pure Orange mixture plus a little Warm White.

4. Using script liner, outline and define a few blossoms with light value from Step 3, thinned with water.

5. With tip of script liner, dot tiny Yellow Citron centers.

Finish

1. Using all-purpose adhesive, attach stars to blue area. Let dry.

2. Apply two or more coats of varnish. Let dry between coats.

Glassware Surface Preparation

1. Wash and dry glassware. Wipe down entire surface with rubbing alcohol and paper towel.

2. Measure down 1" or more from rim. Using painter's tape, mask-off area that will not be painted.

3. Depending on glass size, determine how long stripes will be. Tape-off area below bottom edge of "soon-to-be" stripes.

4. Tape-off sections for stripes, following directions for taping off basket stripes.

Paint the Glassware Design

Stripes:

1. Using ½" flat, paint white stripes with two coats of Wicker White.

2. Paint red stripes with two coats of Engine Red.

Leaves:

1. Using white transfer paper, transfer your choice of images from Patriotic Geraniums Picnic Basket Pattern on page 57 onto glasses.

2. Using #6 flat, fill in leaves with Hauser Green Medium. Let set before shading in center with a corner-load of Green Forest.

3. Pick up a small amount of Berry Wine and add a touch to shadow parts of some leaves.

4. Highlight leaves with a mixture of Fresh Foliage plus a bit of Wicker White.

Geraniums:

1. Using #4 filbert, fill in the geranium shapes with Berry Wine. Let dry for a few minutes.

2. Stroke in a few more defined blossoms with Engine Red.

3. Highlight defined blossoms with a mixture of Engine Red plus Pure Orange plus a bit of Wicker White.

4. Using script liner, dot Berry Wine, then Fresh Foliage centers.

Trim:

1. Using tip of stylus, dot trim with Metallic Gold.

2. Sign your name. Let dry at least 24 hours.

Finish

1. Following manufacturer's directions, place glassware on cookie sheet in cold oven. Turn oven to 350°F; when oven reaches 350°F, set timer and bake for 30 minutes. When time is up, turn off oven and allow glassware to cool for an hour or more before removing from oven.

Geranium Painting Worksheet

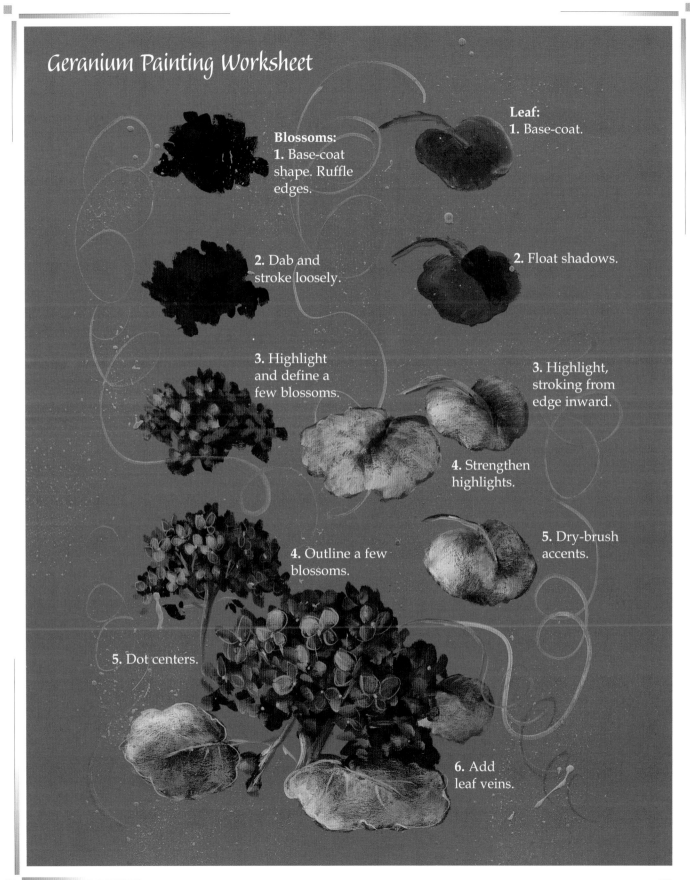

Blossoms:
1. Base-coat shape. Ruffle edges.

Leaf:
1. Base-coat.

2. Dab and stroke loosely.

2. Float shadows.

3. Highlight and define a few blossoms.

3. Highlight, stroking from edge inward.

4. Strengthen highlights.

4. Outline a few blossoms.

5. Dry-brush accents.

5. Dot centers.

6. Add leaf veins.

Twilight Blue Glasses & Bowl

by Rachel Wright

Gather These Supplies

Painting Surfaces:
• Blue glass footed ivy bowl, 5" dia. x 4¾" tall
• Blue glass iced tea glasses, 16 oz.

Enamel Paint Color:
• Pearl White Metallic

Brushes:
• Rounds: #4, #6

Other Supplies:
• Masking tape
• Palette
• Rubbing alcohol
• Soft cloth
• Transfer tools

Surface Preparation

Note: Refer to General Instructions on pages 8–24.

1. Wash and dry glassware.

2. Trace Twilight Blue Patterns onto copy paper. Position traced design inside glass and tape in place. *Notes: There are two designs for the glasses, one for each side.*

The pattern for the bowl repeats all the way around.

3. Wipe surfaces to be painted with rubbing alcohol. Do not touch surface after wiping.

Paint the Design

Notes: Refer to Twilight Blue Painting Worksheet on page 62.

The strokes are painted in blue on the worksheet so that you can see them clearly, but you will be using Pearl White Metallic to paint on the glassware.

1. Use #4 round for smaller strokes and comma strokes, and #6 round for larger strokes.

2. Start at outer, pointed end of each leaf shape and work back toward stem in one smooth stroke with Pearl White Metallic. Touch tip of brush to pointed end of leaf shape. Push bristles flat to widen stroke as you pull down toward the stem, then lift back to the brush tip as you approach the pointed base of the stroke.

3. Paint stems with tip of round brush. Rotate bowl so all strokes will travel in the same direction.

4. Sign your name.

Finish

Note: Refer to Dry & Cure on page 14.

1. Let glasses and bowl dry and cure.

Twilight Blue Patterns

Glasses

Enlarge patterns 200%.

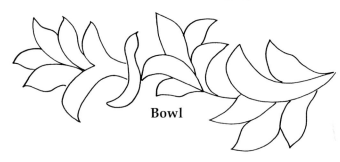

Bowl

Twilight Blue Painting Worksheet

Strokes
1. Push, pull, and lift.

2. Push, pull, and lift.

3. Push, pull, and lift.

Single strokes

Layer strokes

Glass: side one

Glass: side two

Fluted bowl design

RACHEL "04"

Beauty in Flight Pitcher

by Sue Bailey
Photo shown on page 65.

Gather These Supplies

Painting Surface:
• White glazed ceramic pitcher with cobalt blue trim, 6" dia. x 10" tall

Enamel Paint Colors:
• Cobalt
• Hydrangea
• Licorice
• Violet Pansy
• Wicker White

Brushes:
• Flats: #2–#10
• Liner
• Scroller: 10/0
• Sponge
• Stippler: ¾"

Other Supplies:
• Rubbing alcohol
• Soft cloth
• Transfer tools

Surface Preparation

Note: Refer to General Instructions on pages 8–24.

1. Clean pitcher with alcohol. Let dry.

2. Using stippler, dab Wicker White over front of pitcher. Let dry.

3. Transfer Beauty in Flight Patterns on page 64 onto pitcher. Place three large butterflies first — one in front and one on each side. Randomly place ten small butterflies.

Paint the Design

Note: The three large butterflies have the same pattern but different color placement. The ten small butterflies have the same pattern but different color placement.

Butterfly Bodies:

1. Using sponge, base-coat butterfly bodies with Licorice.

2. Highlight with a streak of Wicker White.

Large Dark Blue Butterfly:

1. Base-coat with two or three coats of Cobalt, letting dry between coats.

2. Paint pattern on wings as well as upper teardrop strokes (on Cobalt area) and scallops around edges of wings with Hydrangea.

3. Streak Hydrangea areas with Violet Pansy.

4. Paint teardrop strokes on Hydrangea areas, and all other detail with Licorice. Outline with Licorice.

Large Medium Blue Butterfly:

1. Base-coat with two or three coats of Cobalt plus Wicker White (a medium value blue), letting dry between coats.

2. Paint large pattern on wings as well as upper teardrop strokes (on medium blue area) with Violet Pansy.

3. Lighten Violet Pansy areas in center with dirty brush plus Wicker White.

4. Paint teardrop strokes on Violet Pansy areas, and all other detail with Licorice.

5. Outline with Licorice.

Large Light Blue Butterfly:

1. Base-coat with two or three coats of Hydrangea, letting dry between coats.

2. Paint large pattern on wings as well as upper teardrop strokes (on Hydrangea area) with Cobalt.

3. Using dirty brush, lighten Cobalt areas in center with Wicker White.

4. Add scallops on edge of wings with Violet Pansy.

5. Paint teardrop strokes on Cobalt areas, and all other detail with Licorice.

6. Outline with Licorice.

Small Purple Butterfly:

1. Base-coat with two or three coats of Violet Pansy.

2. Using dirty brush, streak downward on wings to highlight with Wicker White.

3. Paint detail and outline butterfly with Licorice.

Continued on page 64.

Small Blue Butterfly:

1. Base-coat with Cobalt.

2. Using dirty brush, streak downward on wings to highlight with Wicker White.

3. Paint detail and outline butterfly with Licorice.

Small Light Blue Butterfly:

1. Base-coat with Hydrangea.

2. Using dirty brush, streak downward on wings with Cobalt.

3. Paint detail and outline butterfly with Licorice.

4. Sign your name.

Finish

Note: Refer to Dry & Cure on page 14.

1. Let pitcher dry and cure.

Beauty in Flight Patterns

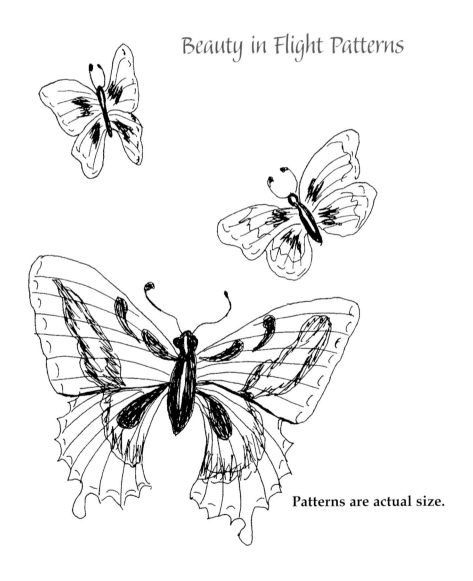

Patterns are actual size.

Tulip Splendor Vase

by Sue Bailey

Gather These Supplies

Painting Surface:
• Tulip vase, 5" dia. x 8" tall

Enamel Paint Colors:
• Butter Pecan
• Green Forest
• Italian Sage
• Midnight
• Violet Pansy
• Wicker White
• Yellow Ochre

Brushes:
• Flats: #2–#10
• Liner
• Scroller: 10/0
• Sponge
• Stippler: ½"

Other Supplies:
• Rubbing alcohol
• Soft cloth
• Transfer tools

Surface Preparation

Note: Refer to General Instructions on pages 8–24.

1. Clean vase with alcohol. Let dry.

2. Using stippler, dab on background with Butter Pecan plus Wicker White. Let dry.

3. Transfer Tulip Splendor Vase Pattern onto front of vase.

Paint the Design

Tulips:

1. Using flats, apply Midnight plus Violet Pansy in dark areas.

2. Using dirty brush, overstroke with Wicker White.

3. Highlight with Wicker White.

Stems & Leaves:

1. Paint stems with Green Forest plus Yellow Ochre.

2. Suggest leaves in background with Italian Sage.

3. While working forward, base-coat leaves with Green Forest.

4. Overstroke with Italian Sage.

5. Add tints of Violet Pansy.

6. Sign your name.

Finish

Note: Refer to Dry & Cure on page 14.

1. Let vase dry and cure.

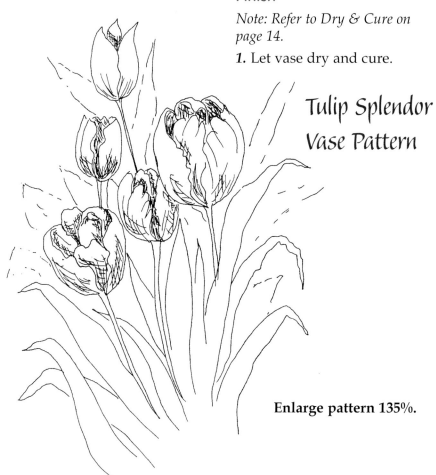

Tulip Splendor Vase Pattern

Enlarge pattern 135%.

Baby Blue & Butterfly Plaque

by Willow

Gather These Supplies

Painting Surface:
- Wooden plaque with carved butterflies

Acrylic Paint Colors:
- Pure Gold (Metallic)
- Violet Pansy
- Wrought Iron

Artists' Pigment Colors:
- Aqua
- Brilliant Ultramarine
- Prussian Blue
- Pure Black
- Raw Umber
- Sap Green
- Titanium White
- Yellow Light

Mediums & Finishes:
- Acrylic sealer, matte
- Artists' varnish, satin
- Blending
- Floating

Brushes:
- Chisel blenders: #2, #4, #6
- High-density sponge roller: 4"
- Liner: 18/0
- Mini mop

Other Supplies:
- Blow dryer
- Brown paper bag without printing
- Sandpaper, medium- grit
- Transfer paper, white
- Transfer tools
- Wood filler

Surface Preparation

Note: Refer to General Instructions on pages 8–25.

1. Prepare wood. Seal wood with varnish plus water (1:1). Let dry.

2. Using sponge roller, base-coat plaque with Wrought Iron.

3. Between each base coat, rub with paper bag.

4. Spray lightly with matte acrylic sealer.

5. Transfer Baby Blue and Butterfly Pattern on page 74 onto plaque.

Paint the Design

Tips for Painting Wings & Tail:

- Apply floating medium to selected area. Side-load #2 chisel blender with shading color and float shadows under each feather where one feather overlaps another. Let dry.

- Reapply floating medium and side-load highlight color. Float highlights on top edge of each feather. Let dry.

- Using liner, thin highlight color to an inky consistency. Paint edges of feather and center shaft line. Let dry.

Tips for Painting Fluffy Feathers:

- Base-coat bird.
- Apply blending gel and rebase-coat the area you are currently working on.

- Wipe brush and base-coat in different values. Place the shading and highlight colors, following growth direction of feathers.

- Wipe brush and blend with chiseled edge. Use short, choppy repetitive strokes. Let dry.

- Glaze to deepen shading and brighten highlights. *Note: It may take several layers of glaze to achieve desired depth.*

- Using a liner, detail with thinned paint.

Tips for Painting Feather Tips:

- Blend with chiseled-edge of brush.

- Follow growth direction.

- Only apply blending gel and paint to an area that can be completed.

- Be certain paint and gel are dry before new layers are added. You may dry each layer of paint with a blow dryer to speed painting time. Spray with matte acrylic sealer. This provides a barrier coat to prevent lifting of the paint layers.

- If blending gel and paint start to dry, do not keep working with it. Let it dry completely. Then add shading and highlighting with glaze.

Continued on page 70.

Refer to Baby Bluebird Painting Worksheet on page 71, Butterfly Painting Worksheet on page 73, and Leaves Painting Worksheet on page 75.

1. Base-coat bird's head and body with Brilliant Ultramarine.

2. Base-coat butterfly with mixture of Aqua plus Brilliant Ultramarine.

3. Base-coat bird's rump with Titanium White.

4. Base-coat bird's beak and feet and butterfly's body with Pure Black.

5. Base-coat leaves and vines with Sap Green. Let dry.

6. Spray with a light coat of matte acrylic sealer. Let dry.

7. Transfer details.

Bird's Eye:

1. Using liner, paint line around pupil with a small amount of Brilliant Ultramarine plus Titanium White. At each end of the eye, pull eye ring outward to form a thin triangle.

2. Paint pupil with thinned Pure Black. Push paint into eye ring, thinning it down if necessary. Let dry.

3. Using handle end of liner, add highlight dot in upper-right corner of eye with Titanium White.

Beak:

1. Using liner, outline edges of beak and highlight down center with thinned Titanium White.

Wings:

1. Apply thin layer of floating medium. Side-load brush with Prussian Blue and shade under each feather separation. Let dry.

2. Apply thin layer of floating medium. Side-load with Aqua and highlight outer edge of each feather.

3. Using liner, paint feather lines with thinned Brilliant Ultramarine plus Titanium White. Add a center shaft line on upper feathers with same mixture.

4. Highlight a few feather and shaft lines with thinned Titanium White.

Head:

Note: Work wet-on-wet and refer to the Growth Direction Diagram when making strokes.

1. Apply a thin layer of blending gel. Rebase-coat head with mixture of Aqua plus Ultramarine Blue. Wipe brush.

2. Using #2 chisel blender, apply Aqua plus Titanium White to crown of head and throat. Dry-wipe brush and use chiseled edge to blend highlight into base coat.

3. Dry-wipe brush and pick up Prussian Blue. Apply shading behind eye, above shoulder, and at nape of neck. Dry-wipe brush and use chiseled edge to work shading color into wet base coat.

Shoulders & Back:

1. Apply a thin layer of blending gel and rebase-coat with Brilliant Ultramarine plus Aqua. Follow growth direction of feathers.

2. While base coat is wet, wipe brush, pick up a small amount of Titanium White on end of chisel blender, and highlight shoulder. Wipe brush and use chiseled edge to blend highlight and base coat.

3. To shade, apply Prussian Blue to back, just above rump. Wipe brush and blend with chiseled edge.

Rump:

1. Apply blending gel and rebase-coat rump with Titanium White. Dry-wipe brush.

2. Apply Raw Umber near body and in a circular area on rump. Dry-wipe brush.

3. Using chiseled edge of small brush, highlight with Titanium White. Using corner of brush, flick Titanium White paint outward over Raw Umber shading. Let dry.

Continued on page 72.

Growth Direction Diagram

Baby Bluebird Painting Worksheet

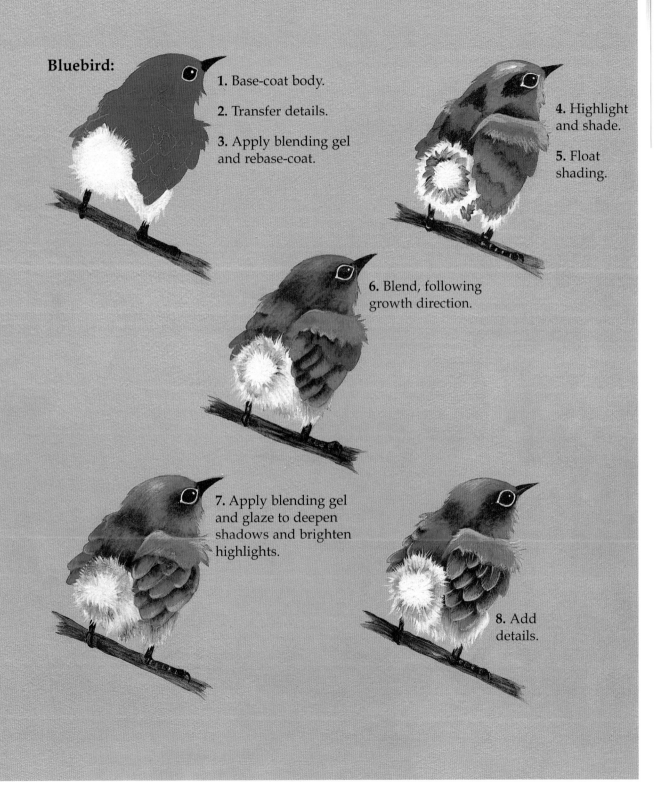

Bluebird:

1. Base-coat body.

2. Transfer details.

3. Apply blending gel and rebase-coat.

4. Highlight and shade.

5. Float shading.

6. Blend, following growth direction.

7. Apply blending gel and glaze to deepen shadows and brighten highlights.

8. Add details.

4. Using liner, add brighter streaks in center of rump with Titanium White. Layer rump highlight like a star with brightest strokes on top in a smaller area.

Feet:

1. Paint feet with Pure Black. While wet, use liner to add Titanium White dots down center of foot.

2. Dry-wipe brush, then tap highlight into black. Let dry.

3. Paint curved segment lines along foot with thinned Pure Black.

Glazing:

Note: Apply a thin layer of blending gel to bird and glaze to reinforce shading and highlighting.

1. Reinforce shading near wing, behind eye, and on back with Prussian Blue.

2. Glaze brighter highlights on crown of head and shoulder area with Titanium White plus Aqua.

Detail:

1. Using liner, add little lines on throat, rump, and shoulder with thinned Titanium White.

2. Using 18/0 liner, add strokes above feathers and at front of shoulder with thinned Titanium White.

Butterfly's Upper Wings:

1. Using #2 chisel blender, apply thin layer of blending gel.

2. Dry-wipe brush, then block in outer section of upper wings with Aqua. Paint midsection with Brilliant Ultramarine. Paint near body with Prussian Blue. Dry-wipe brush.

3. Using chiseled edge, connect colors. Place brush near body of butterfly and drag through all colors toward outer edge of wing with very little pressure. Continuously dry-wipe brush as you streak through colors. *Note: If darker colors take over the wing, wipe brush and pull from outer edge back toward body.*

Butterfly's Lower Wings:

1. Apply a thin layer of blending gel and paint outer sections with Aqua. Paint midsection of lower, or hind, wing with Violet Pansy. Paint section closest to body with Brilliant Ultramarine. Dry-wipe brush. Using chiseled edge, streak through colors. Let dry.

2. Using liner, highlight wings with lines of Titanium White. Add small lines on edges of wings in scalloped sections.

Body & Antennae:

1. Rebase-coat with Pure Black. While wet, stipple a highlight of Titanium White.

2. Using liner, paint antennae with Pure Black. Add a dot of Titanium White on end of each antenna.

Vines:

1. Rebase-coat vines with Sap Green.

2. Using a choppy horizontal motion with chiseled edge of brush, highlight outer edges of vines with Yellow Light, then Titanium White.

3. Float Pure Black shading where vines cross.

Stroke-leaves:

1. Apply blending gel and rebase-coat with Sap Green.

2. While wet, pull accent strokes from outer edge in toward center vein line. Load #6 blender with one of the following colors: Aqua plus Titanium White, Violet Pansy, or Yellow Light and pull strokes from outer edge toward center vein line, decreasing the pressure placed on brush as you pull. Mop to soften accent stroke into leaf. Work quickly.

3. Retransfer vein lines.

4. Apply floating medium and side-load #6 blender with Pure Black. Shade above curve of vein line. Be certain the dark is widest toward base of leaf and tapers as it moves towards tip. Let dry.

5. Apply floating medium. Side-load Pure Black and shade where one leaf covers another.

6. Apply floating medium, blot brush, and side-load Yellow Light. Place highlight under curve of vein line. Mop to soften. Let dry.

7. Using liner, paint vein lines on each leaf with Titanium White plus thinned Yellow Light.

Finishing Details:

1. Paint outer edge and raised borders between routing with Pure Gold. Apply as many coats as needed for a bright, solid coverage, letting dry after each coat.

2. Sign your name. Let dry.

Finish

1. Apply satin varnish.

Butterfly Painting Worksheet

Butterfly:
1. Base-coat body and wings.

2. Apply blending gel and place values.

3. Blend colors. Using chiseled edge of brush, streak through colors.

4. Apply blending gel and glaze.

5. Add details.

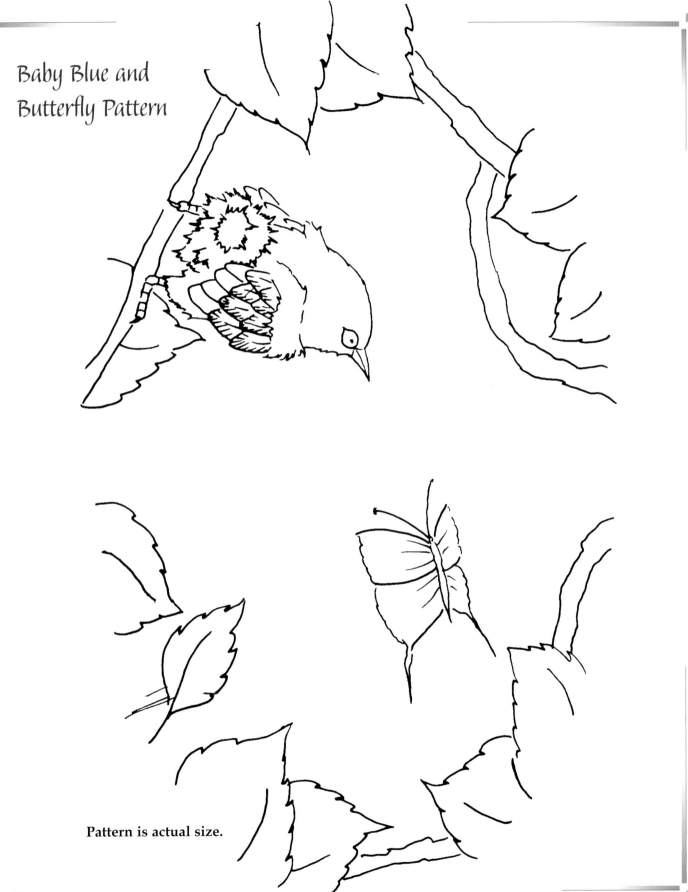

Baby Blue and Butterfly Pattern

Pattern is actual size.

74

Leaves Painting Worksheet

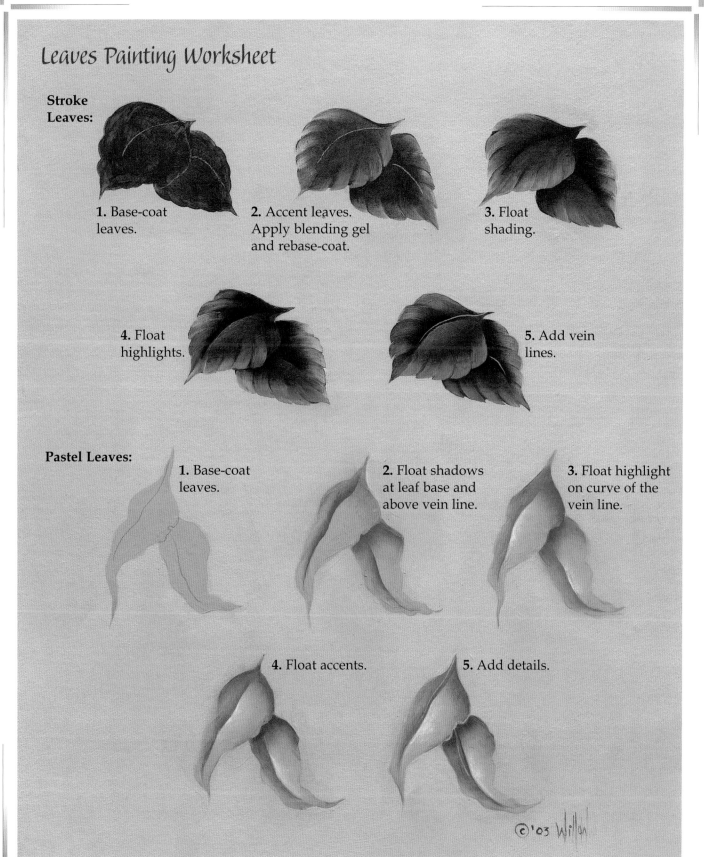

Stroke Leaves:

1. Base-coat leaves.

2. Accent leaves. Apply blending gel and rebase-coat.

3. Float shading.

4. Float highlights.

5. Add vein lines.

Pastel Leaves:

1. Base-coat leaves.

2. Float shadows at leaf base and above vein line.

3. Float highlight on curve of the vein line.

4. Float accents.

5. Add details.

©'03 Willon

Purple Iris Watercolor Painting

by Louise Jackson

Gather These Supplies

Painting Surface:
- 300 lb. rough watercolor paper, acid-free, 9" x 12"

Artists' Pigment Colors:
- Dioxazine Purple
- Hauser Green Dark
- Raw Sienna
- Yellow Light

Acrylic Paint Color:
- Midnight

Brushes:
- Flats: #20 , 1"
- Rounds: #6, #12
- Scruffies: soft, stiff

Other Supplies:
- Blow dryer
- Eraser
- Masking tape
- Palette
- Paper towels
- Pencils
- Salt
- Support board
- Transfer paper: wax-free gray
- Transfer tools
- Water containers

Surface Preparation

1. Mix colors with water on palette before wetting paper. *Note: Acrylics dry darker than they look when wet, watercolors dry lighter.* Wet paper until it is evenly soaked. Allow water to penetrate inside of paper. *Note: The more thoroughly soaked it is, the longer you will be able to work.* Level water so there are no large puddles. Soak up water that might be on table, tape, or support board with a paper towel so it will not run back onto paper.

2. Apply colors with a 1" flat. Start with lightest colors. If you are planning on leaving white paper, leave spaces with little or no color on them. If your light spaces will have tints and shading, allow light colors to bleed into these area or actually apply color here.

3. Soften edges where colors meet with the same 1" flat. Don't blend over each color, just soften at edges. Allow paper and water to do the work by not pushing. Try a stroke, then watch what happens.

Tips:

- As paper dries naturally, it is referred to as the "Damp Stage." Some paintings have leaves or other shapes you may paint on at this stage. They will bleed at edges. When they will no longer bleed at edges, the damp stage is over. However, this does not mean paper is completely dry. Before next layer of painting, dry paper with a blow dryer. It is important for paper to be completely dry, otherwise the water inside the paper may mix with the new water and create blooms or lines that you had not intended.

- In watercolor, when paper begins to loose its shine, it is time to drop salt. When shine is gone and before paper is dry, it is time to spatter water or color. *Note: In acrylics, this technique works best if you sprinkle salt while the paper is still wet.*

Note: Refer to General Instructions on pages 8–24.

1. Transfer Purple Iris Pattern on page 80 onto watercolor paper.

Continued on page 78.

Louise
Jackson MDA

Paint the Design

Note: Refer to Purple Iris Painting Worksheet on page 79.

Flower Petals:

Note: Complete one petal at a time. Refer to Fig. 2 on the Purple Iris Painting Worksheet for color placement on petals.

1. Start with the upper-right petal. Wet one half of petal. Using #12 round, apply Dioxazine Purple. Rinse brush and remove 90% of water. Pull between colors to soften edges.

2. Paint center-left petal. Wet petal. Apply Dioxazine Purple to areas as shown in Fig. 3 of worksheet. Rinse brush and remove 90% of water. Pull brush between colors to soften edges.

3. Repeat this on all petals, placing colors as shown in Fig. 2.

4. Wet petals and complete shading on upper petals by placing Dioxazine Purple according to Fig. 4.

5. To complete shading on center-left petal, place Dioxazine Purple according to Fig. 2. Place additional shading on petal according to Fig. 4. *Note: This shading color is a mixture of Dioxazine Purple and Midnight.*

6. Apply a darker wash of Dioxazine Purple to flipped area of petals.

7. Wet bottom of large front petal. Add in a little thinned Midnight on lower-left as shown in Fig. 4.

8. Paint mixture of Dioxazine Purple and Midnight on dry paper in center of iris between two upper petals.

Beard:

Note: Be certain paper is dry before painting beard sections.

1. Paint in three beard sections by applying Yellow Light on them almost to outside edge as shown in Fig. 3. Leave a little white paper around outside edge.

2. Add in drier Raw Sienna according to Fig. 4.

3. Using #6 round, paint a few tiny growth lines coming out of center beard with Dioxazine Purple.

Stem:

1. Make green mixture of Midnight and Yellow Light. Apply to stem.

2. Lift out color from center of stem by running chiseled edge of a damp #20 flat down center, applying a little pressure.

Leaves:

1. Using #20 flat, apply thinned green mixture on dry paper. Stand brush up straight and use chiseled edge to apply streaks of color to leaf.

2. Quickly rinse brush. Remove 60% of water and pull chiseled end of brush between the color. The paint will run into the water and create streaks.

3. Repeat for all leaves. Using varying intensities of color, make some leaves light and some dark.

4. Paint a little Yellow Light on flipped section of lower-right leaf.

5. Sign your name. Let dry.

Finish

1. Frame as desired.

Purple Iris Painting Worksheet

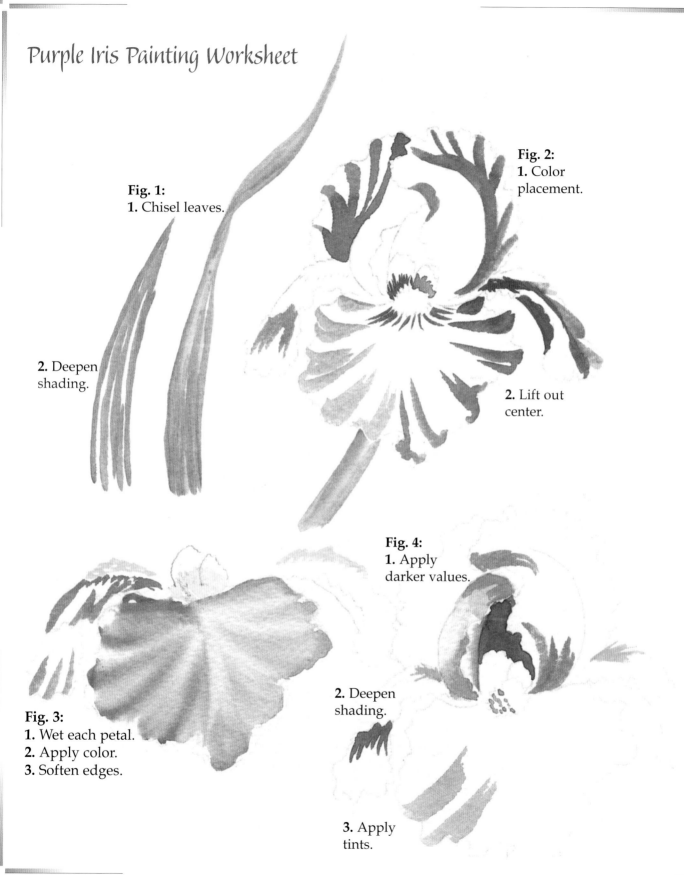

Fig. 1:
1. Chisel leaves.

2. Deepen shading.

Fig. 2:
1. Color placement.

2. Lift out center.

Fig. 4:
1. Apply darker values.

2. Deepen shading.

Fig. 3:
1. Wet each petal.
2. Apply color.
3. Soften edges.

3. Apply tints.

79

Purple Iris Pattern

Enlarge pattern 135%.

Victorian Landscape Plate

by Ginger Edwards
Photo shown on pages 83 & 85.

Gather These Supplies

Painting Surface:
- Wooden plate, 10" dia. with 5¾" base

Acrylic Paint Colors:
- Basil Green
- Cinnamon
- French Vanilla
- Honeycomb
- Ivory White
- Lemonade
- Lime Yellow
- Pure Gold (Metallic)
- Raspberry Wine
- Thicket
- Thunder Blue
- Titanium White

Artists' Pigment Colors:
- Burnt Sienna
- Burnt Umber

Medium & Finish:
- Artists' varnish, finish of your choice
- Floating

Brushes:
- Flats: #10, #12, #14, #20
- Liner: 10/0
- Round: #2
- Scruffy

Other Supplies:
- Cosmetic wedge
- Palette knife
- Sandpaper, fine-grit
- Sea sponge
- Tack cloth
- Transfer tools
- Waxed palette

Surface Preparation

Note: Refer to General Instructions on pages 8–24.

1. Sand surface to remove rough areas. Using tack cloth, remove all traces of sanding dust.

2. Base-coat base of plate with Ivory White. Base-coat remainder of plate with French Vanilla. Two coats may be necessary for a smooth, opaque coverage. Let dry. Sand lightly after each coat.

3. On palette, mix a small amount of Honeycomb with water and floating medium to a transparent consistency.

4. Dampen sponge with water. Squeeze dry. Dab sponge in paint mixture. Using sponge, add texture to French Vanilla areas of plate. *Note: Acrylic paints dry a shade darker than when wet. The texture should be subtle and transparent. A softer effect can be achieved if the surface of the plate is moistened sparingly with water plus floating medium (1:1). Let dry.*

5. Transfer Victorian Landscape Plate Pattern on page 84 onto plate.

Paint the Design

Sky:

1. Use small amounts of paint thinned with water plus floating medium. Moisten surface prior to stroking on paint to aid in blending colors. Using #20 flat, stroke across top of sky with Thunder Blue. Before paint dries, stroke tiny amounts of Raspberry Wine just below blue.

2. Float tiny amounts of French Vanilla behind mountains.

3. Using #10 or #12 flat, paint a few clouds with tiny amounts of Ivory White.

Mountains:

1. Using #12 or #14 flat, paint mountains, with a small amount of Thunder Blue or Thunder Blue plus a bit of Raspberry Wine.

2. Add Titanium White to mixture and highlight mountains.

Water:

1. Moisten surface sparingly with water plus floating medium (1:1) prior to stroking on paint. Using #20 flat, stroke all colors on the water with vertical strokes.

Continued on page 82.

2. Wipe brush and blend lightly horizontally. Repeat colors from sky and mountains. Stroke colors on from darkest to lightest. Let dry.

Trees:

1. Using scruffy, stipple trees on far shore with thinned Thicket.

2. Darken next to ground line with Thicket plus small amounts of Thunder Blue and Burnt Umber.

3. Stipple a few areas with Honeycomb.

4. Highlight with Lemonade plus Lime Yellow.

5. Using liner, paint a few tree trunks or branches with thinned Burnt Umber. Let dry.

Reflections:

1. Moisten surface sparingly with water plus a bit of floating medium. Using flats, add reflections in the water with any sky or foliage colors or mixtures. Stroke paints on with vertical strokes. Blend with light horizontal strokes.

Rose Garland Leaves & Stems:

1. Using liner, paint stems of background leaves with thinned Burnt Umber.

2. Thin Thicket plus Thunder

Blue (1:1) plus a speck of Burnt Umber to a transparent consistency with water plus floating medium. Paint barely visible leaves. Let dry.

Roses:

1. Using #14 flat, paint a circle the size of a rose for each rose with Cinnamon plus a bit of Ivory White.

2. While paint is wet, side-load dirty brush with Raspberry Wine and stroke shading inside throat and across bottom of each rose.

3. Side-load opposite side of brush with Ivory White to stroke petals. Stroke side and back petals that have an upward curve.

4. Stroke side and front petals that have a downward curve. Let dry.

5. Lightly stipple a center in each rose with Raspberry Wine plus Burnt Umber thinned with water to a light value.

6. Add tiny dots of Lemonade for highlights.

Leaves:

1. Using #10 flat, paint leaves with Basil Green. Let dry.

2. Side-load #10 or #12 flat with

Thicket plus Thunder Blue and shade center vein area and outside edges of each leaf. Let dry.

3. Tint some outside edges with the same size brush side-loaded with Raspberry Wine plus Burnt Umber or Burnt Sienna. Tap corner of brush onto leaf to create splotches. Let dry.

4. Using round, flattened while loading, dry-brush highlights on leaves with mixture of Lemonade plus Lime Yellow.

5. Using liner, connect stems to leaves with mixture of Thicket plus small amounts of Burnt Umber and Thunder Blue.

6. Paint veins in leaves with highlight mixture for the center veins and either the highlight mixture or shading mixture for side veins. Paint light veins on dark areas of leaf and darker veins on light areas.

Finishing Details:

1. Using cosmetic wedge, trim edges of plate with Pure Gold.

2. Sign your name. Let dry.

Finish

1. Apply several coats of varnish. Let dry.

Victorian Landscape
Plate Pattern

Pattern is actual size.

Country Charm Plate

by Ginger Edwards
Photo shown on pages 85 & 87.

Gather These Supplies

Painting Surface:
- Wooden plate, 10" dia. with 5¾" base

Acrylic Paint Colors:
- Basil Green
- French Vanilla
- Honeycomb
- Ivory White
- Lemonade
- Lime Yellow
- Pure Gold (Metallic)
- Sunflower
- Thicket
- Thunder Blue
- Titanium White

Artists' Pigment Colors:
- Burnt Sienna
- Burnt Umber

Medium & Finish:
- Artists' varnish , finish of your choice
- Floating

Brushes:
- Filberts: #6, #8
- Flats: #2, #6, #8, #10, #12, #16, #20
- Liner: 10/0
- Round: #2
- Scruffy

Other Supplies:
- Cosmetic wedge
- Palette knife
- Sandpaper, fine-grit
- Sea sponge
- Tack cloth
- Transfer tools
- Waxed palette

Surface Preparation

Note: Refer to General Instructions on pages 8–24.

1. Sand surface to remove rough areas. Using tack cloth, remove all traces of sanding dust.

2. Base-coat base of plate with Ivory White. Base-coat remainder of plate with French Vanilla. Two coats may be necessary for a smooth, opaque coverage. Let dry. Sand lightly after each coat.

3. On palette, mix a small amount of Honeycomb with water and floating medium to a transparent consistency.

4. Dampen sponge with water. Squeeze dry. Dab sponge in paint mixture. Using sponge, add texture to French Vanilla areas of plate. *Note: Acrylic paints dry a shade darker than when wet. The texture should be subtle and transparent. A softer effect can be achieved if the surface of the plate is moistened sparingly with water plus floating medium (1:1). Let dry.*

5. Transfer Country Charm Plate Pattern on page 89 onto plate.

Paint the Design

Sky:

1. Use small amounts of paint thinned with water plus floating medium to a transparent consistency. Moisten surface prior to stroking on paint to aid in blending colors. Using #20 flat, stroke across top of sky with Thunder Blue plus a bit of Burnt Umber. While paint is wet, stroke Ivory White plus a bit of Sunflower near horizon line. Blend while paints are wet.

Background Trees:

1. Using scruffy, stipple trees behind house with a bit of Thicket thinned slightly with water.

2. Stipple a darker mixture of Thicket plus a bit of Burnt Umber and Thunder Blue near ground line.

3. Using liner, paint a few tree trunks and branches with darker mixture. Let dry.

House:

1. Using small flats, paint walls with Titanium White. Let dry.

2. Using side-loaded flats, shade with Burnt Umber plus a bit of Thunder Blue.

3. With #2 flat, indicate windows and door with thinned mixture of Burnt Umber plus Thunder Blue. Let dry.

Continued on page 88.

4. Using small flat, dry-brush highlights on walls sparingly with Titanium White.

5. Using #2 flat and liner, paint roof and chimney with thinned Burnt Sienna. Let dry.

6. Shade with Burnt Sienna plus Burnt Umber.

Ground:

Note: It may be easier to brush and blend paints if surface is moistened lightly with water plus a small amount of floating medium prior to stroking on paint.

1. Using #16 or #20 flat, stroke on ground with Thicket plus a bit of Burnt Umber.

2. Using round, flattened while loading with same thinned mixture, stroke some grass.

3. Using liner, paint additional grass.

Large Tree:

1. Using round and liner, paint tree trunk and branches with Burnt Umber thinned to a light value. Let dry.

2. Stroke additional Burnt Umber plus a bit of Thunder Blue to shade trunk. *Note: No highlights are necessary as the background will show through the transparent paint.*

3. Using scruffy, stipple foliage areas with Thicket thinned to a transparent consistency with water.

4. Stipple darker areas in foliage with a mixture of Thicket plus a bit of Burnt Umber and Thunder Blue thinned with water.

5. Stipple highlights sparingly with Lemonade plus Lime Yellow.

Daisy Garland Stems & Leaves:

1. Base-coat garland with Basil Green; one coat is sufficient. Let dry.

2. Side-load #16 flat with Thicket plus a bit of Burnt Umber and Thunder Blue. Shade next to center on one side and on outside edges of each leaf.

3. Tint some edges with same brush side-loaded with a mixture of Burnt Umber plus Burnt Sienna. Tap corner of brush onto leaf to create splotches. Let dry.

4. Using a round, flattened while loading, dry-brush highlights onto leaf with Lemonade plus Lime Yellow.

5. Paint veins throughout leaves. Use highlight mixture on the center veins.

6. For side veins, use highlight mixture on dark areas of leaves

7. Use shading mixture on any light areas.

Daisies:

1. Using #6 or #8 filbert, stroke petals with a mixture of Thicket plus a bit of Thunder Blue and Burnt Umber thinned to a transparent consistency. Let dry.

2. Using filberts, overstroke petals with Ivory White thinned to a transparent consistency. Let dry.

3. To shade petals, side-load a #16 or #20 flat with Thicket and Thunder Blue (1:1) plus a bit of

Burnt Umber. Position brush with paint side touching center and shade side and back petals next to flower center. Turn brush over and shade tips of side and front petals. Let dry.

4. Paint flower centers with Sunflower. Let dry.

5. Using #6 or #8 flat, shade centers across bottom and shade indentation in center with sideloaded Burnt Sienna plus Burnt Umber.

6. Using liner, paint triangular areas that separate petals near center with Burnt Umber plus a bit of Thunder Blue.

7. Using round, dry-brush highlights on front petals with Titanium White.

8. Using #2 flat, flattened while loading, stroke highlights on side and back petals with Ivory White plus Titanium White.

9. Using liner tip, add texture to flower centers with Sunflower. Highlight centers with Lemonade.

Finishing Details:

1. Using cosmetic wedge, trim edges of plate with Pure Gold Metallic.

2. Sign your name. Let dry.

Finish

1. Apply several coats of varnish. Let dry.

Country Charm Plate Pattern

Enlarge pattern 120%.

French Country Rooster Plate

by PCM Studio

Gather These Supplies

Project Surface:
- Large yellow charger, 13" dia.

Enamel Paint Colors:
- Berry Wine
- Burnt Sienna
- Burnt Umber
- Engine Red
- Fresh Foliage
- Hydrangea
- Lemon Custard
- Licorice
- Periwinkle
- School Bus Yellow
- Warm White
- Yellow Ochre

Medium:
- Enamel clear

Brushes:
- Flats: #4, #8, #10, #12
- Liner: #6
- Script liner: #2

Other Supplies:
- Palette
- Palette knife
- Paper towels
- Petit-four sponge
- Rubbing alcohol
- Spouncers, in various sizes
- Transfer papers: gray, white
- Transfer tools

Surface Preparation

Note: Refer to General Instructions on pages 8–24.

1. Wipe plate with a paper towel saturated with rubbing alcohol. Let dry.

2. Using gray transfer paper, transfer French Country Rooster Patterns on page 92 onto plate.

Paint the Design

Note: Refer to French Country Rooster Painting Worksheet on page 93.

Background:

1. Load a petit-four sponge with enamel clear and pat it around back and breast area of rooster.

2. Dip edge of sponge in Burnt Umber and carefully apply it along back and breast. Pat color into the wet medium to create a graded background around rooster. Let dry.

Rooster's Body:

1. Using #6 liner, undercoat rooster's body and wing with Yellow Ochre. Apply two coats to get an opaque coverage.

2. Undercoat comb and wattle with Engine Red. Let dry.

3. Load large flat with enamel clear, side-load with Burnt Sienna. Apply shading around wing and up back of rooster. Apply shading to backs of legs and where they join the body.

4. Using #6 liner, stroke wing with Engine Red.

5. Shade comb and wattle with Berry Wine.

6. Using #6 liner, highlight comb and wattle with School Bus Yellow plus a bit of Engine Red. Add more yellow and repeat process. Finish with some brighter yellow highlights.

7. Paint beak with Burnt Umber. Highlight with Hydrangea while paint is wet.

Rooster's Tail Feathers:

1. Using #6 liner, stroke tail feathers with Periwinkle. Paint two comma-stroke tail feathers with Engine Red. Paint remaining feathers with Lemon Custard.

2. Restroke blue feathers with a double-loaded brush of Hydrangea and Periwinkle.

3. Restroke yellow feathers with a double-loaded brush of Engine Red and Lemon Custard.

4. Overstroke red feathers with School Bus Yellow, then with Lemon Custard.

5. Restroke top tail feather with a double-loaded brush of Fresh Foliage and Hydrangea. Overstroke feather with fresh Foliage plus Lemon Custard.

Continued on page 92.

French Country Rooster Patterns

Enlarge patterns 180%.

Rooster Details & Highlights:

1. Using #6 liner, highlight body with Lemon Custard.

2. Add additional highlights with Sunflower.

3. Paint eye with Licorice. Highlight with warm White.

4. Add feet with Burnt Sienna.

5. Add detail to wing, painting long lines an scalloped shapes with Licorice. Outline and add dots with Lemon Custard.

6. Load sponge with enamel clear. Touch edge with Burnt Umber. Pat shading where tail feathers join the body and add just a bit around the wing.

Border:

1. Paint large S-strokes with Periwinkle.

2. Add thin lines with Hydrangea.

3. Paint comma strokes with Hydrangea. Overstroke with Periwinkle.

4. Paint dots with Engine Red.

5. Sign your name.

Finish

Note: Refer to Dry & Cure on page 14.

1. Let plate dry and cure.

French Country Rooster Painting Worksheet

Rooster:
1. Base-coat.

2. Shade rooster.

3. Fill in wings.

4. Highlight.

5. Add additional highlights.

6. Add details.

Petite Posies Teapot

by Sonja Richardson

Gather These Supplies

Painting Surface:
- White glazed china teapot

Enamel Paint Colors:
- Baby Pink
- Butler Magenta
- Evergreen
- Fresh Foliage
- Hydrangea
- Periwinkle

Medium:
- Enamel clear

Brushes:
- Flats: #2, #8
- Round: #2

Other Supplies:
- Pencil
- Rubbing alcohol
- Soft cloth

Surface Preparation

Note: Refer to General Instructions on pages 8–24.

1. Wipe teapot with rubbing alcohol. Dry thoroughly.

2. Refer to Posies Painting Worksheet as a guide for size of design in relation to your teapot. Using pencil, make tiny guide marks for wavy garland around teapot just above bottom of handle and spout. Make light marks on teapot above roses to indicate positions of tiny tulips.

Paint the Design

Garland:

1. Using #8 flat, pitty-pat Fresh Foliage to form a background for garland.

2. Using #2 flat, paint a pair of roses at each dip in garland with Baby Pink. Shade with Butler Magenta.

3. Using round, paint three teardrops with Hydrangea below each pair of roses. Shade with Periwinkle.

4. Using #2 flat, paint groups of three checkers below highest parts of garland with Butler Magenta.

5. Paint single-stroke leaves with Evergreen on garland background between roses.

Upper Floral Pattern:

1. Using #2 flat, paint tiny tulips with Baby Pink and shade with Butler Magenta.

2. Paint a stem and two leaves for each tulip with Evergreen.

Lid:

1. Alternate roses and three-checkers designs around lid.

2. Using round, paint two teardrop-shaped leaves above each pair of roses with Evergreen.

3. Wash Butler Magenta plus enamel clear on two raised round areas on knob of lid.

4. Wash Evergreen plus enamel clear on lower portion of the raised leaf.

5. Sign your name.

Finish

Note: Refer to Dry & Cure on page 14.

1. Let teapot dry and cure.

Posies Painting Worksheet

Posies:
1. Base-coat.
2. Shade.

Foliage:
1. Base-coat.

2. Shade foliage.

3. Pitty-pat foliage.

Pansy Bouquet Ceramic Teapot

by Helen Stadter

Gather These Supplies

Painting Surface:
- White glazed china teapot

Enamel Paint Colors:
- Berry Wine
- Burnt Sienna
- Dioxazine Purple
- Fresh Foliage
- Lemon Custard
- Licorice
- Metallic Pure Gold
- Periwinkle
- School Bus Yellow
- Thicket
- Warm White

Medium:
- Enamel clear

Brushes:
- Blender mop
- Flats: #2, #4, #6
- Round: #4
- Script liner: 20/0
- Stippler

Other Supplies:
- Paper towels
- Rubbing alcohol
- Soft cloth
- Transfer papers: gray, white
- Transfer tools

Surface Preparation

Note: Refer to General Instructions on pages 8–24.

1. Wipe teapot with rubbing alcohol. Dry thoroughly.

2. Using blender mop, stipple rim, handle, spout, bottom edge of teapot, and rim of lid with Periwinkle. Keep paint thin and dry by stippling first on a paper towel. *Note: This will avoid heavy patches; it should be airy.*

3. Stipple over Periwinkle with brush-mixed Fresh Foliage and Thicket for a soft gray green. Do not wash brush between colors; just wipe on a paper towel.

4. Stipple over main area of teapot with Thicket, then with Periwinkle, and finally with Lemon Custard around outer edges. *Note: You should see each color in the background.* Keep darkest, heaviest area in middle and let colors fade outward from design area. Let dry.

5. Using white transfer paper, transfer main lines of Pansy Bouquet Ceramic Teapot Patterns on page 99 onto both sides of teapot. Repeat pansy pattern around lid.

Paint the Design

Note: Paint main design on both sides of teapot. When highlighting and shading pansies refer to the Pansy Bouquet Teapot Shading & Highlighting Diagram on page 98 as a guide.

Yellow Pansy:

1. Base-coat each petal with Warm White. Keep it thin, with no ridges. Let dry, then retransfer pattern details with gray transfer paper.

2. Base-coat each petal with Lemon Custard, following contour of each petal.

3. Moisten #4 flat with enamel clear. Side-load with Burnt Sienna. Float between back petals to separate. Float on large front petal around throat. Add some color to outer edges. Soften, avoiding harsh edges.

4. Deepen shading with Berry Wine at triangular areas or where petals come from center.

5. Moisten #4 flat with enamel clear. Dip into Warm White and highlight edges of each petal. Randomly highlight large front petal. Pull strokes toward center to create veins.

6. Add tints of School Bus Yellow.

7. Base-coat center with Lemon Custard. Shade at top with Burnt Sienna.

8. Using script liner, paint linework with paint thinned with enamel clear and a bit of water. Paint with Berry Wine and Burnt Sienna, following petal's contour. Keep linework thin and delicate.

9. Add comma strokes at center with Warm White.

Continued on page 98.

Purple Pansy:

1. Base-coat petals with mixture of Dioxazine Purple, Warm White, and a touch of Burnt Sienna, following contour of petals.

2. Moisten brush with enamel clear and side-load with Dioxazine Purple. Float between petals to separate and shade. Add Berry Wine for variety.

3. Deepen triangular areas and next to center with Dioxazine Purple and Licorice.

4. Highlight edges of petals with base-coat mixture plus Warm White. Pull strokes toward center, following contour of petals.

5. Add tints of Periwinkle plus Warm White.

6. Paint center same as yellow pansy, except use Licorice for detail linework.

Two-color Pansy:

1. Follow instructions for Yellow Pansy on page 96 for upper half, and Purple Pansy for lower half, using same colors and techniques.

Buds:

1. Paint buds same as Yellow Pansy. *Note: Vary yellows for interest.*

Stems & Leaves:

1. Base-coat stems and leaves with light wash of Thicket. Keep stems light in value.

2. Side-load Thicket and shade leaves any place a leaf is behind a flower or where leaves overlap one another, also at stem edge, down bottom side of leaf, and down vein line. Paint vein with thinned Thicket. *Note: Do not place vein exactly in center of leaf. It is usually offset to one side or the other so it does not cut leaf in half. Do not pull vein to tip of leaf.*

3. Deepen triangular areas with Dioxazine Purple and Thicket.

4. Using enamel clear medium, side-load Fresh Foliage and highlight leaves and stems on top side and down vein line. Repeat with Lemon Custard and Warm White, then with Fresh Foliage and Lemon Custard, varying highlights for interest.

5. Add tints of brush-mixed Periwinkle and Warm White, then Berry Wine and Burnt Sienna.

Finishing Details:

1. Using #4 round, paint strokework trim with Pure Gold.

2. Sign your name.

Finish

Note: Refer to Dry & Cure on page 14.

1. Let teapot dry and cure.

Pansy Bouquet Teapot Shading & Highlighting Diagram

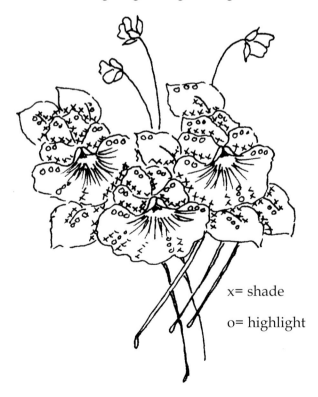

x= shade

o= highlight

Pansy Bouquet Ceramic Teapot Patterns

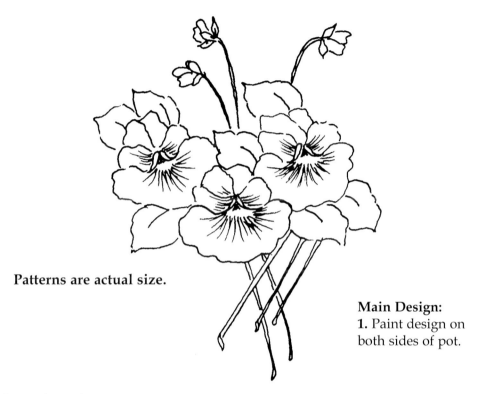

Patterns are actual size.

Main Design:
1. Paint design on both sides of pot.

Strokework on rims

Strokework on lid & handle

Lid

Deer Tin Pockets

by Mary McCullah

Gather These Supplies

Painting Surfaces:
- Hanging rusty tin pocket, varied sizes (2)

Acrylic Paint Colors:
- Basil Green
- Peony
- Tangerine
- Terra Cotta

Artists' Pigment Colors:
- Burnt Sienna
- Burnt Umber
- Ice Blue Dark
- Ice Green Light
- Pure Black
- Raw Sienna
- Sap Green
- Warm White

Medium & Finish:
- Artist's varnish, matte
- Blending

Brushes:
- Dome round, medium
- Filbert: #2
- Flat: #2
- Liner: 10/0

Other Supplies:
- Palette
- Paper towels
- Soft cloth
- Transfer tools

Surface Preparation

Note: Refer to General Instructions on pages 8–24.

1. Wipe tin pockets with a damp cloth.

2. Trace and transfer Deer Patterns on page 105 onto pockets. *Note: On small design, do not transfer markings on the butterfly or all of the grass blades.*

Paint the Design

Fur Painting Tips:
- Stroke in growth direction.
- Match length of stroke to length of fur.
- Value color change is necessary to create a realistic fur look.
- To achieve fine lines, thin paint. Use blending gel plus a touch of clean water for fine lines such as whiskers and fur pulled out into the background.

Background:

Notes: The technique involves using the dome to dry-brush small amounts of paint and create a soft multicolored background.

Work small sections at a time, remembering to let colors continue from one side of an antler to the other for continuity. Begin on right side of head.

1. Place Burnt Sienna, Ice Blue Dark, Peony, Tangerine, and Terra Cotta on a palette.

2. Pick up a small amount of Terra Cotta and softly scrub into surface. Dry-wipe brush and pick up Tangerine, letting the two colors soften together.

3. Use Burnt Sienna to work further out into background letting it simply soften into the rusty tin. Continue to dry-wipe brush. If it becomes necessary to clean the brush, be certain to squeeze out all moisture between paper towels.

4. Add Peony to brighten background, especially behind the center of the head and antlers. Continue technique until entire background is completed.

5. Accent with Ice Blue Dark under chin area. Use same method and colors for the small pocket, adding some Basil Green as an accent in grass areas.

Larger Pocket:

Refer to Deer Painting Worksheet on page 103.

Note: The first layer of paint may be a little transparent; more than one layer may be required (for example, the chin.)

Continued on page 102.

Left Ear:

1. Using filbert, paint in lightest area on rim and area of hair that pulls into the ear with Ice Green Light.

2. Inside top of ear place Burnt Sienna plus Ice Green Light, working downward into Burnt Umber plus Ice Green Light, then Burnt Umber.

3. Paint back of ear with gray tones of Burnt Umber plus Pure Black plus Warm White and Burnt Umber plus Ice Green Light.

Right Ear:

1. Paint inside center of ear with pink mixture, working outward into Burnt Umber plus Ice Green Light and placing Burnt Umber at darkest area inside ear.

2. Using liner, paint rim with Burnt Umber at bottom, changing to Ice Green Light at top.

3. Paint back of ear with gray mixture, adding Burnt Umber for dark accents and Ice Green Light along top outside edge.

Light Fur Areas:

1. Using filbert, paint chin, muzzle, neck area, and lower bridge of nose with Ice Green Light.

Antlers:

Note: Using very little paint on a dry brush, work with a light value of Ice Green Light, a medium value of Burnt Umber plus Ice Green Light, and dark values of Burnt Umber plus Raw Sienna and Burnt Umber. Do one antler section at a time. Start with light value and work other colors into it.

1. Using dirty filbert, lay colors in overlapping strokes. Brush-stroke marks are valuable since antlers are rough.

2. Separate antler from background and add form with Ice Blue Dark on edge of some of the darker areas.

3. Dry-brush Tangerine in lighter areas.

Eye:

1. Using filbert, place a small amount of Burnt Umber at top of eye area, working downward. Toward bottom of eye, let tin show to create a glow.

Tip of Nose:

1. Double-load filbert with Ice Blue Dark and Pure Black. Place blue color across top of nose and around right nostril opening.

2. Fill in leftover areas with Pure Black.

Dark Area on Muzzle & Chin:

1. Using filbert, paint dark marking on side of muzzle and on chin with Pure Black.

2. Fill in nostril opening with Pure Black.

Lip & Mouth:

1. Using liner, paint lip with Pure Black.

2. Paint a faint line on top of Black at front of lip with Ice Blue Dark.

Head:

Note: Using filbert, begin at top of head. Place overlapping strokes in one small area at a time, letting colors softly merge.

1. Place Ice Green Light on light area at top of head, working into Raw Sienna. Use Burnt Umber plus Raw Sienna in dark areas.

2. Add gray accents with Ice Blue Dark.

3. Begin back of neck behind ear with Ice Green Light, working into Raw Sienna, then Burnt Umber plus Raw Sienna.

4. On lower portion of bridge of nose, work Burnt Umber plus Ice Green Light upward to meet existing color.

5. Using very little paint, scrub off bottom edge of neck into the tin.

Antler Details:

1. Using filbert, reset values to increase intensity. Use Ice Green Light, Ice Green Light plus Raw Sienna, and Burnt Umber.

2. Using liner, detail base of right antler with some Pure Black and Ice Green Light plus Raw Sienna. Pull some lines up the antler to create ridges and make small smudges to indicate bumps. Let dry.

3. Dry-brush Tangerine plus Warm White in lightest areas. Dry-brush Ice Blue Dark on darker edges.

Left Ear Details:

1. Using filbert, reset dark inside ear with Burnt Umber.

2. Add some Ice Green Light plus Burnt Umber for a medium value and add a touch of Ice Blue Dark on outer edge.

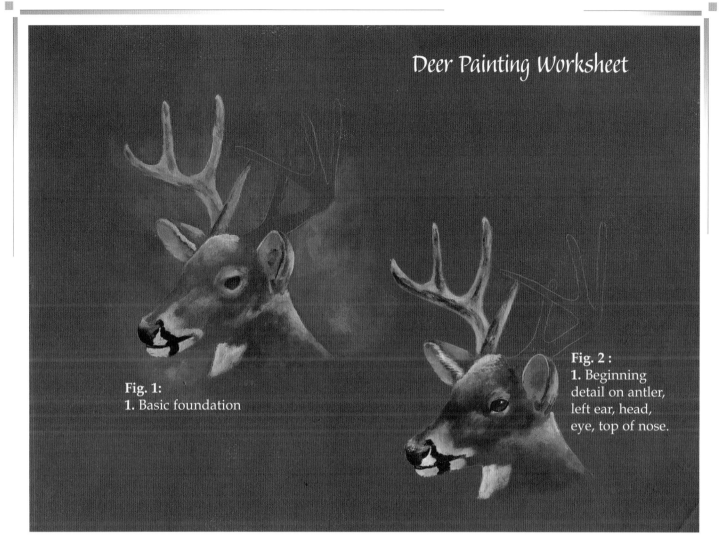

Fig. 1:
1. Basic foundation

Fig. 2 :
1. Beginning detail on antler, left ear, head, eye, top of nose.

3. On back of ear, reset dark value with Burnt Umber. Use Warm White plus Tangerine for lightest area.

4. Using liner, pull down hairs from rim with Warm White. Thin paint with blending gel plus a touch of water.

Right Ear Details:

1. Strengthen pink inside ear with Burnt Sienna plus Warm White.

2. Darken center area with Burnt Umber.

3. Using liner, accent inside rim with Burnt Umber.

4. Paint small hairs pulled off left side of ear with thinned Burnt Umber, Warm White plus Burnt Umber, and Warm White.

5. On right side, use Warm White for short hairs.

6. Detail back of ear with Burnt Umber to deepen dark areas. Use Burnt Umber plus Green Ice Light for a medium value and Tangerine plus Warm White for a light value.

Eye Details:

1. Using blending gel and liner, reset dark at top of eye with a touch of Pure Black. Work this downward carefully to retain the glow at the bottom.

2. While still wet, create a glow in highlight area with Ice Blue Dark and softly blend.

3. Add a sharp highlight in this area with Tangerine plus Warm White.

4. Use thinned Pure Black sparingly under eye and across top of eye.

5. Pull a touch of Burnt Umber plus Warm White lightly across top of eye for the illusion of a lid.

Continued on page 104.

Head Details:

Note: Using filbert, intensify values to create good form. With a small amount of blending gel and paint, use a technique much like Antlers on page 102.

1. Use Tangerine plus Warm White for light on top of head, working into Burnt Umber plus Warm White, and Raw Sienna plus Warm White.

2. Work Burnt Umber plus Raw Sienna and Burnt Umber into darker areas.

3. Lighten over and under eye with Burnt Umber plus Warm White.

4. Lighten further over eye with Warm White.

5. Paint bridge of nose mostly with Burnt Umber. Add hint of light on left side of bridge of nose with Ice Blue Dark.

6. Use some Ice Blue Dark for gray tones in front of eye and a touch of Black plus Burnt Umber in darkest area around eye.

Light Fur Area Details:

1. Using filbert, lighten light fur areas around muzzle and chin with Warm White.

2. To merge these areas with brown areas next to them, double-load brush with Warm White and Warm White plus Burnt Umber. Stroke this between two value areas.

3. Shade throat area with Raw Sienna plus Warm White and a touch of Ice Blue Dark.

Tip of Nose Details:

1. Using filbert, reset light portion with Ice Blue Dark and blending gel.

2. Dry-wipe and soften into some wet Pure Black.

3. Using side of liner, add a sparkle of Warm White.

Finishing Details:

1. Dry-brush final highlights on top of head with Warm White plus Tangerine and Warm White.

2. Use this same process on back of neck and over eye with filbert.

3. Using liner, pull fine hairs from edge of chin, with thinned Warm White.

4. Add whiskers with thinned Burnt Umber.

Finish

1. Varnish and let dry.

Smaller Pocket   Antler:

1. Paint, following the Antlers instructions on page 102.

Flower & Bud:

1. Using #2 flat, base-coat flower and bud with Green Ice Light.

Leaves:

1. Double-load #2 flat with Basil Green and Sap Green and stroke in leaves, leaving a striped appearance.

Butterfly:

1. Using #2 flat and liner, base-coat wings and body with Ice Blue Dark.

Grasses:

1. Using 10/0, begin pulling a foundation area for the detail grasses with thinned Burnt Umber plus Sap Green.

Antler Details:

1. Add a shadow under antler with Burnt Umber plus Pure Black thinned with blending gel.

Flower & Bud:

1. Using #2 flat and blending gel, reset Ice Green Light.

2. Dry-wipe brush. Shade with Basil Green. Highlight with Warm White.

3. Add accents of Tangerine toward petal edges.

4. In blossom center, use liner to pull Burnt Umber stamens with dots of Tangerine on ends.

Grass:

1. Using liner, pull more grasses with thinned Pure Black plus Sap Green.

2. On right side, add light grasses with Basil Green plus Tangerine plus Warm White.

3. On left side, use only Basil Green.

Butterfly:

1. Lighten wings a little with Ice Green Light. Let dry.

2. Freehand detail with thinned Pure Black.

3. Add markings of Burnt Sienna plus Tangerine on bottom wing.

4. Lighten back of butterfly's body with Ice Green Light.

5. Paint legs, eye, and antennae with thinned Pure Black.

Finishing Details:

1. Add further detailing or shading to leaves, if necessary.

2. Check darkest areas of antlers and deepen, if needed.

3. Sign your name. Let dry.

Finish

1. Varnish and let dry.

Deer Patterns

Patterns are actual size.

Two Blues Still Life on Tin Tile

by Rhonda Cable

Gather These Supplies

Painting Surfaces:
- Rusted tin ceiling tile, 12" sq.
- Wooden frame, 12" sq.

Acrylic Paint Colors:
- Blue Ribbon
- Icy White
- Light Gray
- Linen
- Medium Gray
- Tapioca
- Thunder Blue
- Wrought Iron

Artists' Pigment Colors:
- Indian Blue
- Light Red Oxide
- Pure Black
- Raw Sienna
- Titanium White
- Van Dyke Brown

Medium & Finish:
- Acrylic sealer, matte
- Crackle

Brushes:
- Flats: #2, #6, #8, #12, ½", ¾", 1"
- Rounds: 20/0, 10/0, 5/0, 3/0, 2/0, #0, #1
- Liners: 10/0, 5/0, #0
- Old toothbrush

Other Supplies:
- Blow dryer
- Palette
- Transfer tools

Surface Preparation

Note: Refer to General Instructions on pages 8–24.

1. Transfer Two Blues Pattern on page 110 onto ceiling tin.

2. Base-coat table with Linen (do not paint pail). Let dry.

3. Transfer board lines to table. *Note: The skirt runs horizontal so there is no need for these lines.*

4. Apply thin coat of crackle medium to table, following direction of boards. Do not apply to pail area. On table rim, apply crackle medium vertically, then apply horizontally on skirt. Dry with blow dryer.

5. Using #6 flat, apply Tapioca to areas with crackle medium. Paint each individual board and its rim separately. Paint in direction boards run (vertically on edge and horizontal on skirt.) Do not backstroke.

6. Dry with hair dryer. Cracks will form as topcoat dries.

7. Paint frame with same colors and procedures as the table, including a crackled finish. Let dry.

8. Using liner, "distress" frame with Van Dyke Brown. "Miter" corners with paint, making that paint stroke a bit wider to give the impression that it was not a good miter.

9. Using toothbrush, spatter with Van Dyke Brown. Set frame aside.

Paint the Design

Table:

1. Side-load an ever-so-slightly damp ¾" flat with Van Dyke Brown and shade under table lip. *Note: Do not play with it too much or it will lift off the paint on top of crackle medium.*

2. Using liner, enhance cracks, divisions, and add knot holes with Van Dyke Brown. Dry-brush Van Dyke Brown along boards to add texture.

Continued on page 108.

Pail:

Refer to Two Blues Painting Worksheet on page 109.

1. Base-coat inside of pail with Light Gray.

2. Shade inside pail along outside edge with dry-brushed Medium Gray.

3. Dry-brush Titanium White highlights at top of inside of bucket under rim.

4. Using liner, base-coat handle with Wrought Iron. Let dry.

5. Dry-brush highlights with Light Gray.

6. Base-coat rim of pail with Pure Black. Let dry.

7. Dry-brush highlights of Light Gray.

8. Using damp flat, apply rust around inside rim with a mixture of Light Red Oxide plus Raw Sienna (1:1). Apply small amounts of paint to pail along rim. Using clean damp brush, soften edges.

9. Base-coat outside of pail, painting around handle brackets with Indian Blue. Let dry.

10. Dip a damp 5/0 liner into Titanium White paint and blend on palette to work paint into bristles. Randomly apply "run" marks (drips) on pail. *Note: Applying pressure while pulling brush downward will vary the width of the "runs."* Let air dry.

11. Add chips in enamel around base and lip with Wrought Iron plus a bit of Pure Black.

12. Around outside edges of chips, dry-brush Icy White (brush away from chip.) Dry-brush centers of larger chips with Light Red Oxide plus Raw Sienna.

13. Outline around handle bracket with Wrought Iron, applying more pressure on the right side.

14. Base-coat lower section of bracket with Indian Blue. Base-coat the top section of bracket with Wrought Iron. Dry-brush a highlight of Icy White where Indian Blue and Wrought Iron meet.

15. Side-load damp 1" flat with Thunder Blue. Shade left side of pail, making initial stroke just inside pattern line. Make second stroke right up to edge. Blend color out until it disappears. Dry with blow dryer. If it is not dark enough, repeat.

16. Dry-brush highlight with Icy White on the opposite side but slightly toward center.

Blueberries:

1. Base-coat blueberries with Blue Ribbon.

2. Shade the left side of each berry with Thunder Blue.

3. Dry-brush highlights on the right side of each with Icy White.

4. Base-coat blossom marking with Wrought Iron. Highlight left sides of blossom markings with Icy White.

Shadows:

1. Side-load a damp 1" flat with Wrought Iron. Place brush up against edge of pail and pull color away from pail, fading as you go.

2. Using #6 flat, paint shadows of berries in same manner.

3. Sign your name. Let dry.

Finish

1. Spray tile and frame with matte acrylic sealer. Let dry.

2. Install tile in frame.

Two Blues Painting Worksheet

Pot:
1. Base-coat all areas.

2. Chip in enamel around lip and base. Dry-brush centers of chips.

3. Apply "run" marks randomly. Apply rust marks along rim.

4. Dry-brush highlights on rim and handle.

5. Base-coat berries.

6. Detail berries.

7. Shade bucket on left side.

8. Dry-brush highlight on right side of bucket.

9. Shade inside of bucket.

Two Blues Pattern

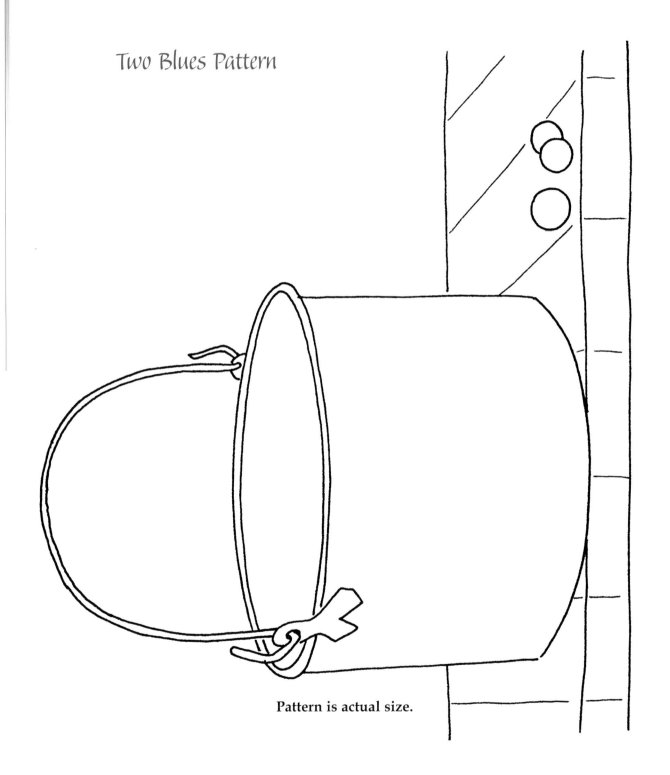

Pattern is actual size.

Daisy & Bumblebee Card

by Cindy Mann Vitale
Photo shown on pages 113.

Gather These Supplies

Painting Surfaces:
- 140 lb. watercolor paper, acid-free, 4¾" sq.
- Black specialty paper, 6½" sq.
- Heavy paper, 6¹¹⁄₁₆" x 13⁵⁄₁₆"
- White paper, 4¾" sq.
- Yellow specialty paper, 6⅞" sq.

Artists' Pigment Colors:
- Burnt Umber
- Pure Black
- Yellow Ochre

Papier Paint Colors:
- Cobalt Blue
- Disco (glitter)
- Fresh Foliage
- Licorice
- School Bus Yellow
- Sunflower
- Thicket
- Wicker White

Medium:
- Papier flow

Brushes:
- Flats: #6, #8, #10
- Liners: #0, #1
- Old toothbrush
- Rounds: #0, #1, #2, #3, #5, #6, #8
- Wash: ¾", 1"

Other Supplies:
- Deckled-edged scissors
- Double-sided foam adhesive circles, ¼" dia.
- Permanent black ink pen, #005
- Rubber cement
- Transfer tools

Surface Preparation

Notes: Refer to General Instructions pages 8–24.

The daisy is two separate layers of paper. The first layer is glued so petals are loose. The second layer is mounted so petals float.

1. Using Daisy & Bumblebee Pattern on page 112, transfer checkerboard edge and flower stem but not any interior details onto 4¾"-square paper. This will serve as center panel.

2. Transfer two daisies onto yellow paper that you will cut out later.

3. Cut a deckled edge around black paper.

4. Score and fold heavy paper in half to form a 6¹¹⁄₁₆"-square card.

Paint the Design

Daisies:

Note: Paint both daisies in their entirety even though they are stacked, because it will be possible to see sections of the one underneath.

1. Paint petals with Wicker White. Shade with diluted Licorice.

2. Paint center with Sunflower. Shade with Yellow Ochre.

3. Paint around outside edge of flower center with Burnt Umber.

4. Add dimensional dots with Licorice around the center.

Center Panel:

1. Base-coat flower stem with Fresh Foliage. Shade with Thicket.

2. Brush thin wash of Cobalt Blue inside square in upper half.

3. Paint bee's black stripes with Licorice.

4. Paint bee's yellow areas with Sunflower. Shade with Yellow Ochre.

5. Paint wings with thinned Wicker White to achieve a translucent look.

6. Paint over wings with Disco.

7. Base-coat corners of checkerboard edge with Sunflower. Shade with Yellow Ochre.

8. Paint corner design with large dot of Licorice. Add dots of Wicker White around center. Let dry.

9. Dot School Bus Yellow in Licorice centers.

Continued on page 112.

Finishing Details:

1. Using pen, draw linework and details.

2. Using toothbrush, spatter daisies, center design, and yellow paper with Pure Black.

Finish

1. Secure black paper to center of yellow paper with rubber cement. Let dry.

2. Add dimensional dots on yellow paper with Licorice. Let dry completely.

3. Secure center design to black paper.

4. Secure center of one daisy. The petals should be moveable.

5. Attach remaining daisy on top of first daisy with an adhesive circle.

Daisy & Bumblebee Pattern

Pattern is actual size.

Flying Flower Gourd Wind Chime

by Aurally Cone

Gather These Supplies

Painting Surface:
- Gourd, 6" dia. x 8" high

Acrylic Paint Colors:
- Bayberry
- Blue Ink
- Clay Bisque
- Green Meadow
- Licorice
- Light Periwinkle
- Periwinkle
- Winter White
- Wrought Iron

Artists' Pigment Colors:
- Raw Sienna
- Sap Green
- Van Dyke Brown
- Yellow Light

Finishes:
- Acrylic sealer, matte
- Artists' varnish, satin
- Painter's finishing wax

Brushes:
- Filbert: #4
- Flat: 1"
- Liner: 20/0

Other Supplies:
- Bamboo wind chimes, small
- Black permanent marking pen
- Drill & ¼" bit
- Dust mask
- Jigsaw or saber saw
- Palette
- Paper towels
- Pencil
- Ruler
- "S" hook
- Safety goggles
- Sea sponge
- Steel wool, #0000
- Transfer tools
- Wood filler

Constructing a Wind Chime

1. Clean outside of gourd.

2. Mark a line horizontally around gourd at 8" length from the top.

3. Wearing safety goggles and dust mask, cut off bottom portion with saw. Clean out inside. Fill holes or blemishes with wood filler and wipe off excess with a damp paper towel. Drill a hole in top of gourd for hanging.

4. Restring wind chime. Gather cords and tie them in a large knot to prevent gourd from sliding down.

5. When wind chime top is sealed, pull strings from the chime up into the gourd, passing them through the hole at the top.

6. Attach an "S" hook to cord and knot it.

Surface Preparation

Note: Refer to General Instructions pages 8–25.

1. Using sponge, pounce entire gourd with Sap Green, then with touches of Wrought Iron. Let some natural color of the gourd show through especially along bottom edge. Let dry.

2. Transfer outline of butterfly and leaves from Flying Flower Wind Chime Pattern on page 117. Repeat pattern on back.

3. Base-coat butterflies with Clay Bisque.

4. Sponge in background for flowers with Blue Ink. Let dry.

Paint the Design

Leaves:

1. Base-coat leaves with Bayberry. *Note: The edges of the leaves are jagged.*

2. Shade outside edges of leaves with Green Meadow.

3. Float leaf veins with Green Meadow. *Note: This will be a back-to-back float, leaving a center gap.*

Hydrangeas:

1. Place Light Periwinkle, Periwinkle, and Winter White on palette. *Note: The hydrangea flower is made up of many small blooms. Using #4 filbert, begin single-stroking petals of blooms. Shade areas with Periwinkle, then gradually add touches of Winter White. As you reach the middle of the cluster, add Periwinkle to Light Periwinkle. The top of the cluster is Winter White with Light Periwinkle. Leave a center on some of the

Continued on page 116.

blooms. Also have some partial blooms showing. Let dry.

2. Add center dots with a mixture of Winter White plus Yellow Light on lightest blooms. Add dots of Light Periwinkle to darkest blooms. *Note: Not all blooms will have centers showing.*

3. Shade behind large flower clusters with a mixture of Wrought Iron plus a touch of Van Dyke Brown. *Note: Also use this mixture behind butterflies to bring them forward.*

Butterflies:

1. Recoat butterflies with Yellow Light. Let dry.

2. Transfer fine details of butterflies.

3. Base-coat dark edging with Licorice, but not fine-line detailing. Add small dots along edge with Yellow Light. Add two small dots at bottom with Light Periwinkle.

4. Highlight outer edge of butterfly with Yellow Light.

5. Using marking pen, add detailing on wings and body.

6. Shade body area and under fold of upper wing with Raw Sienna.

7. Add antennae with Licorice plus a bit of Winter White.

8. Sign your name. Let dry.

Finish

1. Spray inside of gourd with matte acrylic sealer. Let dry.

2. Seal outside with varnish. Let dry.

3. For a special glow, apply finishing wax. Let dry.

4. Buff with steel wool.

5. Assemble wind chime according to directions.

Wind Chime Assembly Diagram

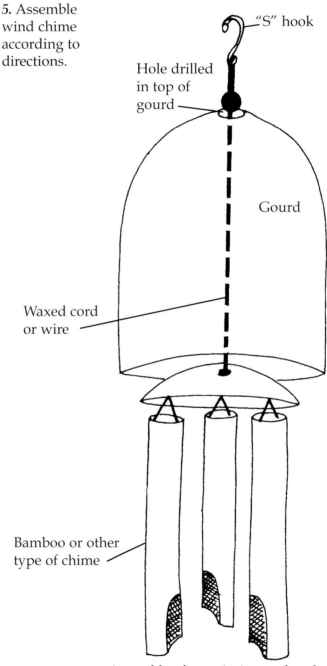

"S" hook

Hole drilled in top of gourd

Gourd

Waxed cord or wire

Bamboo or other type of chime

Assemble after painting and sealing. Place chimes far enough in the gourd that the tops are not seen.

Flying Flower Wind Chime Pattern

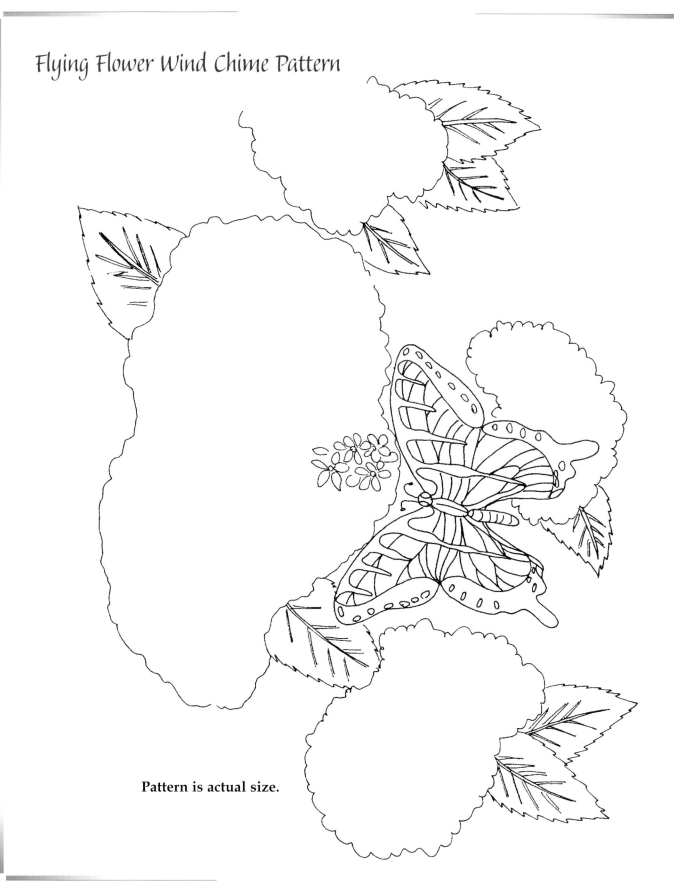

Pattern is actual size.

Candy Canes Gift Jar & Tag

by Karen Popp

Gather These Supplies

Painting Surfaces:
- Cardstocks:
    white 6" x 3¾", 3" x 4"
    red 1¾" x 3½"
- Quart canning jars (2)
- Wooden candy canes,
    1⅜" long (2)
- Wooden jar top, 3¾" dia.
    with 2¹³⁄₁₆" routed area

Acrylic Paint Colors:
- Alizarin Crimson
- Real Brown
- Wicker White

Enamel Paint Colors:
- Berry Wine
- Burnt Umber
- Engine Red
- Fresh Foliage
- Thicket
- Wicker White

Papier Paint Colors:
- Engine Red
- Wicker White

Mediums & Finish:
- Acrylic sealer, matte
- Enamel clear
- Papier flow

Brushes:
- Flats: #2, #6, #12
- Liners: #1, #2
- Round: #2
- Script liner: 10/0
- Scruffy: ¾"

Other Supplies:
- Cocoa mix with mini
    marshmallows
- Glitter
- Hemp cord
- Hole punch
- Hot-glue gun & glue sticks
- Masking tape
- Pine garland, 14" long
- Red satin ribbon, ¼" wide
- Red/white striped grosgrain
    ribbon, 1" wide
- Rubbing alcohol
- Ruler
- Scissors
- Soft cloth
- White texturizing paint
- White tissue paper

Surface Preparation

Notes: Refer to General Instructions on pages 8–24.
    Use acrylic paints with Candy Cane Patterns on page 122.

Jar:

1. Clean jar with alcohol. Let dry.

2. Copy and position Candy Cane Patterns inside jar. Tape in place.

3. Stuff jar with white tissue to provide an opaque painting surface.

Jar Top:

1. Paint underside of jar lid with Real Brown.

2. Paint outside of jar lid with Wicker White. Let dry. Set aside.

Tag:

1. Fold white cardstock in half for a 3" x 3¾" card with fold at left side. Set aside.

Paint the Design

Notes: Refer to Christmas Painting Worksheet on page 121.
    Use enamel paints.

Candy Canes:

1. Base-coat candy canes with Wicker White. Let dry. Apply a second coat. Let dry.

2. Shade with Burnt Umber and enamel clear. Let dry.

3. Using #6 flat, paint stripes with Engine Red.

4. Using #1 liner, shade stripes with Berry Wine. Highlight with Wicker White.

Continued on page 120.

Holly:

1. Base-coat holly leaves with Thicket. Let dry.

2. Highlight leaves with Fresh Foliage.

3. Tint leaves with Engine Red.

4. Using script liner, paint tendrils with Fresh Foliage plus Thicket.

5. Paint dots on berries with Berry Wine and Engine Red.

Peppermints & Rickrack:

1. Position and tape peppermint candy pattern inside jar.

2. Base-coat peppermints with Wicker White. Let dry.

3. Shade peppermints with Burnt Umber and enamel clear on left side. Let dry.

4. Using #2 flat, paint stripes on peppermints with Engine Red. Let dry.

5. Using script liner, highlight candies with Wicker White.

6. Connect candies together in a rickrack design with Thicket.

Snow & Dots:

1. Using scruffy, pounce Wicker White from top down to 1½" from the top and from bottom of the jar up to 1½" from bottom.

2. Add random dots on jar with Wicker White.

Jar Top:

Note: Use acrylic paints.

1. Paint peppermint candy stripes on jar lid with Alizarin Crimson. Let dry.

2. Using #2 script liner, highlight stripes with Wicker White. Let dry.

3. Apply two coats of matte acrylic sealer.

Tag:

Note: Use papier paints.

1. Applying paint from bottle, draw rickrack border around front of 3" x 4" white cardstock with Engine Red, slightly in from edge of card.

2. Mix Engine Red plus flow medium (1:1). Using #12 flat, paint diagonal candy cane stripes 1" apart.

3. Using liner, paint two narrow lines on white stripes with Engine Red. Let dry.

4. Trim painted cardstock to measure approximately 2" x 3". Round corners.

5. Applying paint straight from bottle, paint a border line around red cardstock near edge with Wicker White.

6. Paint rims of candy canes with Wicker White. Let dry.

7. Applying Wicker White straight from bottle, fill in front of candy canes to give dimension. Let dry.

8. Paint candy-cane stripes with Engine Red. Highlight with Wicker White. Let dry.

9. Position painted striped cardstock centered on white card front and secure in place with clear-drying glue. Position red cardstock centered on striped cardstock and glue in place.

10. Hot-glue candy canes in a crossed position on center red cardstock.

11. Punch hole for hanging tag in upper-left corner.

12. Tie a small bow with red ribbon and glue in upper-left corner.

Finish

1. Fill jar with cocoa mix and mini marshmallows. Wrap striped grosgrain ribbon around neck of jar, overlap ends, and hot-glue to secure.

2. Place lid on jar. Hot-glue pine garland around jar top. Add "snow" to garland with white texturizing paint. While wet, sprinkle with glitter.

3. Thread hemp cord through hole in card and tie around neck of jar.

Christmas Painting Worksheet

Candy Cane:

1. Base-coat.

2. Shade along inside.

Peppermint:

3. Add stripes.

4. Shade and highlight.

Holly:

1. Base-coat holly.

2. Base-coat and highlight berries.

3. Highlight foliage.

Christmas Plaid:

1. Base-coat.

2. Add stripes.

3. Add stripes.

4. Add stripes.

Snow Scene:

1. Base-coat.

2. Shade.

3. Highlight

4. Spatter.

Candy Cane Patterns

Enlarge patterns 135%.

Winter Scene Patterns

Patterns are actual size.

Winter Scene Gift Jar & Tag

by Karen Popp
Photo shown on pages 125.

Gather These Supplies

Painting Surfaces:
- Cardstocks:
  cream 3" x 3", 2⅛" x 1½" oval
  dark green 5¼" x 2½"
- Quart canning jar with ring
- Wooden jar topper for lid,
  3" dia.

Acrylic Paint Color:
- Real Brown

Enamel Paint Colors:
- Berry Wine
- Burnt Umber
- Engine Red
- Licorice
- Thicket
- Warm White
- Wicker White
- Yellow Ochre

Papier Paint Colors:
- Berry Wine
- Burnt Umber
- Dark Hydrangea
- Engine Red
- Thicket
- Wicker White

Mediums:
- Enamel clear
- Papier flow

Brushes:
For glass & ceramics:
- Flats: #2, #6, #12, ¾"
- Liners: #1, #2
- Scruffy: ¾"

For wood:
- Flats: #2, #6, #12
- Liner: #1
- Round: #2
- Script liner: 10/0
- Spackle brush
- Toothbrush

Other Supplies:
- Chalk, contrasting with white
- Clear-drying glue
- Craft knife
- Floral tape
- Glitter
- Hemp cord
- Hole punch
- Hot-glue gun & glue sticks
- Masking tape
- Rubbing alcohol
- Ruler
- Scissors: craft, decorative-
  edged
- Soft cloth
- Transfer tools
- White texturizing paint
- Wire

Items for jar top:
- Burgundy pillar candle, 3" dia.
- Grapevine wreath, 3" dia.
- Miniature fir trees, 1" high (1),
  2" high (2)
- Miniature sled, approx. 1½"
  long
- Potpourri
- Red checkered fabric,
  1½" x 11½'"

Surface Preparation

Note: Refer to General Instructions pages 8–24.

Jar:

1. Clean jar with alcohol.
Let dry.

2. Trace Winter Scene Patterns on page 122. Position and tape inside jar.

3. Using scruffy, pounce in oval with Warm White. Let dry.

4. Remove pattern from jar. On back of pattern, trace pattern lines with a contrasting color of chalk. Position pattern, right side up, over oval and tape in place. Trace pattern lines to transfer chalk onto oval.

Continued on page 124.

Top:

1. Paint wood topper with Real Brown. Let dry.

Tag:

1. Fold green cardstock into a 2⅝" x 2½" card.

Paint the Design

Note: Use enamel paints.

House:

1. Base-coat house with Berry Wine.

2. Shade with Burnt Umber.

3. Base-coat door with Yellow Ochre and shade with Burnt Umber.

4. Base-coat windows with Licorice. Outline and define panes with Warm White.

5. Base-coat roof with Wicker White and shade with Burnt Umber.

Trees & Road:

Note: Refer to Christmas Painting Worksheet on page 121.

1. For background trees, brush-mix Thicket, Warm White, and enamel clear medium. Using #2 flat, pounce foliage.

2. Paint foreground trees with Thicket. Highlight with Warm White.

3. Paint road with Burnt Umber thinned with clear medium.

Branches & Berries:

1. Paint bare-branch bushes with Burnt Umber.

2. For berries, add dots of Engine Red to branches.

Snow:

1. Shade snow with brush-mixed Burnt Umber, Thicket, and enamel clear.

2. Using toothbrush, spatter entire jar with Wicker White plus enamel clear.

Tag:

Note: Use papier paints.

1. Mix Thicket plus flow medium (1:1). Using #12 flat, paint vertical lines on cream cardstock. Let dry. Paint horizontal lines. Let dry. Trim with decorative-edged scissors to measure approximately 2½" x 2¼".

2. Paint with wash of Dark Hydrangea plus flow medium on oval cream cardstock. Paint border with Berry Wine.

3. Using #2 flat, pounce on trees with a brush-mix of Thicket and Wicker White. Let dry.

4. Using paint from bottle tip, add dimensional snow with white texturizing paint. Let dry.

5. Shade with Burnt Umber plus papier flow. Let dry.

6. Paint bare-branch bush with Burnt Umber. Add Engine Red dots for berries. Let dry.

7. Mix Wicker White plus flow medium (1:1). Using toothbrush, spatter oval cardstock.

8. Position painted green-plaid cardstock centered on dark green card (cut and folded in preparation section) and glue in place. Position painted oval cardstock centered on green-plaid cardstock and glue in place.

9. Punch hole in upper-left corner for hanging tag.

Finish

1. Secure candle in jar with floral tape. Fill around bottom of candle with potpourri.

2. Place wooden lid on jar. Hot-glue sled and trees in place on lid.

3. Using spackling brush and white texturizing, cover lid with "snow." Also paint some inside sleigh.

4. Glue 1" tree inside sleigh. Sprinkle "snow" with glitter. Let dry.

5. Fold under edges of fabric strips, to a width that fits rim of lid. Wrap fabric strip around lid rim, overlap ends on back side of jar and hot-glue to secure.

6. Wind 3" grapevine wreath loosely around rim of jar lid. Wire together to secure ends.

7. Thread hemp cord through hole in card and tie around neck of jar.

Metric Equivalency Charts

mm-millimeters   cm-centimeters
inches to millimeters and centimeters

inches	mm	cm	inches	cm	inches	cm
⅛	3	0.3	9	22.9	30	76.2
¼	6	0.6	10	25.4	31	78.7
½	13	1.3	12	30.5	33	83.8
⅝	16	1.6	13	33.0	34	86.4
¾	19	1.9	14	35.6	35	88.9
⅞	22	2.2	15	38.1	36	91.4
1	25	2.5	16	40.6	37	94.0
1¼	32	3.2	17	43.2	38	96.5
1½	38	3.8	18	45.7	39	99.1
1¾	44	4.4	19	48.3	40	101.6
2	51	5.1	20	50.8	41	104.1
2½	64	6.4	21	53.3	42	106.7
3	76	7.6	22	55.9	43	109.2
3½	89	8.9	23	58.4	44	111.8
4	102	10.2	24	61.0	45	114.3
4½	114	11.4	25	63.5	46	116.8
5	127	12.7	26	66.0	47	119.4
6	152	15.2	27	68.6	48	121.9
7	178	17.8	28	71.1	49	124.5
8	203	20.3	29	73.7	50	127.0

yards to meters

yards	meters	yards	meters	yards	meters	yards	meters	yards	meters
⅛	0.11	2⅛	1.94	4⅛	3.77	6⅛	5.60	8⅛	7.43
¼	0.23	2¼	2.06	4¼	3.89	6¼	5.72	8¼	7.54
⅜	0.34	2⅜	2.17	4⅜	4.00	6⅜	5.83	8⅜	7.66
½	0.46	2½	2.29	4½	4.11	6½	5.94	8½	7.77
⅝	0.57	2⅝	2.40	4⅝	4.23	6⅝	6.06	8⅝	7.89
¾	0.69	2¾	2.51	4¾	4.34	6¾	6.17	8¾	8.00
⅞	0.80	2⅞	2.63	4⅞	4.46	6⅞	6.29	8⅞	8.12
1	0.91	3	2.74	5	4.5	7	6.40	9	8.23
1⅛	1.03	3⅛	2.86	5⅛	4.69	7⅛	6.52	9⅛	8.34
1¼	1.14	3¼	2.97	5¼	4.80	7¼	6.63	9¼	8.46
1⅜	1.26	3⅜	3.09	5⅜	4.91	7⅜	6.74	9⅜	8.57
1½	1.37	3½	3.20	5½	5.03	7½	6.86	9½	8.69
1⅝	1.49	3⅝	3.31	5⅝	5.14	7⅝	6.97	9⅝	8.80
1¾	1.60	3¾	3.43	5¾	5.26	7¾	7.09	9¾	8.92
1⅞	1.71	3⅞	3.54	5⅞	5.37	7⅞	7.20	9⅞	9.03
2	1.83	4	3.66	6	5.49	8	7.32	10	9.14

Editor: Mickey Baskett

Staff: Jerry Mucklow, Lenos Key, Diannne Miller, Karen Turpin, Ellen Glass, Sylvia Carroll, Phyllis Mueller, Mary Williams, Deena Haney

Plaid Products

Acrylic Paint Colors:

Aspen Green 646
Autumn Leaves 920
Basil Green 645
Bayberry 922
Blue Ink 642
Blue Ribbon 719
Bluebell 909
Butter Pecan 939
Buttercream 614
Cinnamon 913
Clay Bisque 601
English Mustard 959
French Vanilla 431
Fresh Foliage 954
Gray Green 475
Green Meadow 726
Honeycomb 942
Icy White 701
Indigo 908
Ivory White 427
Lemonade 904
Licorice 938
Light Gray 424
Light Periwinkle 640
Lime Yellow 478

Linen 420
Medium Gray 425
Midnight 964
Nutmeg 944
Olive Green 449
Patina 444
Peony 518
Periwinkle 404
Plum Pudding 934
Pure Gold (Metallic) 660
Purple 878
Purple Passion 638
Raspberry Wine 935
Real Brown 231
Settlers Blue 607
Silver Sterling (Metallic) 662
Sunflower 432
Tangerine 627
Tapioca 903
Terra Cotta 433
Thicket 924
Thunder Blue 609
Vintage White 515
Violet Pansy 440
Wicker White 901
Winter White 429
Wrought Iron 925

Artists' Pigment Colors:

Alizarin Crimson 758
Aqua 481
Brilliant Ultramarine 484
Burnt Carmine 686
Burnt Sienna 943
Burnt Umber 462
Dioxazine Purple 463
Green Umber 471
Hauser Green Dark 461
Hauser Green Light 459
Ice Blue Dark 235
Ice Green Light 233
Indian Blue 236

Light Red Oxide 914
Medium Yellow 455
Napthol Crimson 435
Phthalo Green 50
Prussian Blue 486
Pure Black 479
Pure Orange 628
Raw Sienna 452
Raw Umber 485
Red Light 629
Sap Green 458
Titanium White 480
Turner's Yellow 679
Van Dyke Brown 504
Warm White 649
Yellow Citron 503
Yellow Light 918
Yellow Ochre 917

Enamels:

Autumn Leaves 4005
Baby Pink 4003
Berry Wine 4007
Burnt Sienna 4014
Burnt Umber 4012
Butler Magenta 4004
Butter Pecan 4011
Cobalt 4025
Dioxazine Purple 4030
Engine Red 4006
Evergreen 4036
Fresh Foliage 4019
Green Forest 4021
Hauser Green Medium 4041
Hunter Green 4020
Hydrangea 4024
Italian Sage 4023
Lemon Custard 4017
Licorice 4032
Metallic Gold 4033
Metallic Silver Sterling 4034
Midnight 4026

Pearl White Metallic 4045
Periwinkle 4027
Pure Orange 4008
School Bus Yellow 4016
Thicket 4022
Violet Pansy 4029
Warm White 4002
Wicker White 4001
Yellow Ochre 4015

Papier Paints:

Berry Wine 1724
Burnt Umber 1728
Cobalt Blue 1738
Dark Hydrangea 1739
Disco (glitter) 1754
Engine Red 1726
Fresh Foliage 1737
Licorice 1744
School Bus Yellow 1733
Sunflower 1732
Thicket 1734
Wicker White 1721

Painting Mediums:

Artists' Varnish 885
Blending Gel Medium 867
Clear Medium 4035
Floating Medium 868
Flow Medium 1769
Glazing Medium 693
Papier Flow Medium
Wash Medium 698

Index